The Eagle of the Canavese

The Eagle of the Cavavese

Franco Balmamion
and the Giro d'Italia

Herbie Sykes

The Eagle of the Canavese

First published in 2008 by:

Mousehold Press		Sport and Publicity
Victoria Cottage		75 Fitzjohns Avenue
Constitution Opening	and	Hampstead
Norwich NR3 4BD		London, NW3 6PD
www.mousehold-press.co.uk		www.sport&publicity.co.uk

Reprinted in 2011

ISBN 978 1 874739 49 4 (Paperback)
ISBN 978 1 874739 50 0 (Hardback)

Cover design: Adam Wilks

Printed by CLE Print, St Ives, Cambridgeshire

Publishers' note

We have published a number of books about some of the significant names in cycling's past – biographies of Tom Simpson, Jacques Anquetil and Miguel Induraín – and more recent popular riders such as Allan Peiper. However, when Herbie Sykes approached us with an idea for a book about Franco Balmamion and his triumph in the 1962 Giro d'Italia this was clearly a very different proposition. Here was a writer we'd never heard of and a rider who was barely known to English readers. Balmamion may well have won the Giro twice, but his is not a name that readily springs to mind when great cycling champions are talked about. Then we took one glance at the manuscript and it immediately told us that this was no standard cycling biography.

Of course, *The Eagle of the Canavese* is a biography of this little known Italian cyclist; furthermore, much of the narrative is rooted in one particularly spectacular edition of the Giro d'Italia which, against all the odds, he won, but the book is so much broader in its scope than that. In the first place the author introduces us to a colourful host of other cyclists, those Balmamion rode with and against. These and other characters involved in professional road racing reflect not just the cycling, but the political and social climate of Italy in the 1960s. Most of these Herbie has recently interviewed to bring the reader up to date with these heroes and villains of Balmamion's era, some whose careers ended in contentment, and others in the sad wistfulness of lost opportunities. What also gives this book its breadth as well as making it so contemporary is that it offers vigorous comment on the ethics of sport, and of cycling in particular, and draws some trenchant comparisons between then and the present day.

Herbie Sykes writes with an easy expertise and an engaging passion. This, and his love of the country, the cycling and, especially, the people who make up this story is all apparent. And was so in our first reading of the manuscript. None of this detracts from the honesty of the book, as getting to the truth of things seems a primary concern of the author in his endeavour to recover Franco Balmamion from oblivion and secure for him the recognition he deserves. It is a worthy endeavour and one in which we believe he has succeeded fully.

CONTENTS

Part One – The Origin of the Species

Part Two – The 1962 Giro d'Italia

Part Three – The Silent Champion

Author's acknowledgements
I wish to thank all the cyclists and cycling people who gave their time freely: Franco and Rosanna, the Peracino family, Adrian, Richard, Mecu, Dan, Patrick, Adam, Gianni and Simone, Angelo Marello, le Signore Giacotto, the Vai family, Fausto Coppi, Don Quixote, the fine people at 114 and the Sykes's. Thanks also to Justin, Tone and Cheesey for offering such meagre support as they could muster in my role as President. It's been an honour and a privilege.

Dove andiamo Pera?

Photographic acknowledgements
We would like to thank the following for allowing us to use photographs from their private collections: Antonio Bailetti, Franco Balmamion, Germano Barale, Nino Defilippis, Donatella Giacotto, Walter Martin, Imerio Massignan, Bruno Mealli, Guido Neri, Mario Peracino.

Publishers' acknowledgements
We would like to express our thanks to Mick Clark, Patti, Amanda, the Seans, Frank the Q, Extraordinary Dave, Duffers, Phil Liggett, Luke DB, Alex, Phil O'Conner, Dave Reed and Steve Cummings and the guys for their help and inspiration. And, of course, Herbie Sykes for first showing us that manuscript.

Franco Balmamion, Vigorelli Velodrome, Milan

PART ONE

THE ORIGIN OF THE SPECIES

THE FORGOTTEN MAN

The most extraordinary thing about Mecu is his unbreakable, bloody-minded straightforwardness. It has always seemed to me that the more abstractive and complex the task, the greater his pleasure in simplifying it, distilling it down to rudiments and getting it done with minimal fuss. He's one of the more remarkable people I know, and Piedmontese to his very marrow

The Piedmontese, surrounded on three sides by the great Alps and forever mindful of the twin imperatives of landscape and climate, are unusual Italians in that they are not generally given to excesses of talking, which is to say to blather and to equivocate. Thus my having tentatively enquired, at midday on 3rd August 2005, Mecu had by 12.47 scheduled a meeting with a former professional cyclist whom he'd never met, his fellow Piedmontese Franco Balmamion, twice winner of the Giro d'Italia, the Tour of Italy.

Before his 24th birthday Balmamion won successive Giros (or *Giri* as Italians have it) in 1962 and 1963, a feat which (improbably, as yet another doping scandal emerges around the 2007 edition of the race) no Italian cyclist has been able to emulate in almost half a century since. Several genuine greats of the sport – Felice Gimondi, Francesco Moser and Marco Pantani amongst them – have tried and failed, for the Giro is invariably tougher, more hazardous and less formulaic than its more celebrated, more moneyed counterpart – the Tour de France. Only two foreigners, Eddy Merckx and the formidable Spaniard, Miguel Induráin, the greatest champions of their respective generations, have successfully defended the Giro d'Italia.

And yet, curiously, in a sport where the exploits of most grand tour winners are legion, virtually nothing is known of Franco Balmamion outside of Piedmont, let alone Italy. I wanted to know why a cyclist good enough to have beaten riders held to be amongst the greatest ever to have competed, in arguably the worlds hardest bike race, has seemingly been air-brushed from the history of the sport.

Piedmont, the mountainous northern Italian region which has the great baroque city of Turin as its administrative centre, borders France to the west, Switzerland to the north west. The area is for the most part extraordinarily beautiful, unyielding and largely desolate, its terrain and seasons harsh and unforgiving. The Piedmontese, as befits a mountain people, are understated, resolute and resourceful. It's always seemed to me that their DNA contains a quiet pragmatism seldom found elsewhere in Italy where, in the main, the journey, particularly the linguistic journey, from A to B is best undertaken … well, circuitously. For the majority of Italians, particularly those of the centre and south, the journey itself is, of course, of infinitely greater import than the destination. Italians love nothing more than the seduction of conversation, the endless foreplay of their richly textured, beautifully aesthetic language. They habitually and skilfully talk about nothing in particular, and in particular they seem possessed of a unique and innate ability to find things to talk *around*. For a practical demonstration simply visit a Southern Italian bank or municipal office on a quiet day and ask a simple question. Assuming you have time – preferably a lot of it – to kill…

I first met Domenico 'Mecu' Beccaria in April 1991, in Solo Toro, the elegant souvenir shop of his beloved Torino Calcio, the tragic, fabled 'second' football team of Turin. A group of four of us had seen fit, inexplicably it still seems, to take a 24- hour train ride from Northern England (in pre budget-airline Britain a veritable bargain at £273; British Airways were charging, if memory serves, over £400) to watch the Turin Derby – Torino versus the mighty Juventus. Satellite TV had begun to show Italian football, and it was wonderfully, impossibly glamorous. We were young and slightly misguided and had decided that we deserved a weekend away from the turgid, mindless basket case that in those heady days was English football in general, and Manchester City in particular.

Romantic, delusional fools that we were, it rather appeared that it would be a good idea to align ourselves with an Italian version of City, a kind of stylised, deluxe version if you will. Toro ticked all the boxes: overshadowed by an all-powerful, big, Northern 'industrial' city rival; neurotic supporters; morally bankrupt leadership; and, most importantly of all, utterly incapable of putting a foot right on the field. Moreover, Toro proudly draws its support almost exclusively from Turin and the surrounding Piedmont region, while 'Juve', owned and bankrolled by the Agnelli family, owners of FIAT and Italy's most powerful industrialists, has become a type of Italian Manchester United – corpulent, powerful, and overwhelmingly successful. But it wasn't ever thus.

The 'Grande Torino' of the mid to late 1940s was, by common consent, the greatest sporting team Italy has known. Champions for four consecutive seasons between 1946 and 1949, 'La Granata' – so called because their kit was coloured the deep red of the pomegranate – boasted virtually the entire national team amongst their number. Alongside the great cyclists Fausto Coppi and Gino Bartali, Toro became a symbol of hope and pride for a country psychologically and collaterally crippled by the war.

It's an over simplification – but emphatically true – to state that pre-war Italy was a nation, and a people, intrinsically unsuited to military conflict of any sort, let alone to the carnage visited upon it by Mussolini's egocentric, bungling alliance with Hitler. Hitherto a collection of proud City states and Kingdoms, Italy had been unified in 1861 under the Piedmontese Savoy Monarchy, but remained riven by complex and to this day largely intractable regional insecurities and schisms, and in particular by a profound but amorphous North–South divide. Still reeling from a disastrous and specious war in Abyssinia, poor, disparate Italy had no collective stomach for a fight it could never hope to understand, let alone win. As such when, in June 1946, a referendum resulted in the rejection of the moribund Savoy dynasty and to the establishment of an Italian republic, the peninsular was given a second bite of the cherry. Now a fragile but very real sense of nationhood emerged from the wreckage.

During the immediate post-war years and alongside the Grande Torino, Coppi and Bartali, both conquerors of the previously unwinnable – for an Italian* – Tour de France, were the embodiment of a feeling that, though battered and bruised, Italy could shake off her chronic inferiority complex. Finally the country found a cause behind which it could unite – and utterly divide, such was the intensity of the rivalry between her two greatest sporting champions, Coppi and Bartali. Coppi was flamboyant, divorced, Piedmontese and agnostic, an unwitting symbol of the 'New Italy' – mechanised, industrialised and socially fluid. By contrast, Bartali, much the more popular of the two, was devout, stoical and Tuscan, the very personification of Catholic piety, the very antithesis of Fausto Coppi.

---

* Prior to Bartali in 1938, Ottavio Bottecchia was the only Italian to have won the Tour, in 1924 and 1925.

In Italy, one's allegiance to either Coppi or Bartali and the values and ideologies they were held to represent, carried a significance well beyond mere 'fandom'. During the post-war period *everything* was politicised and everybody, regardless of whether they were for cycling, was for either the younger *Campionissimo* Coppi (broadly speaking in the red corner, representative of a new, more liberal Italy) or, more likely, for the brave old lion Bartali, fighting out of the Christian Democrat blue, preserver of the faith and torch carrier for conservatives, true believers, underdogs and traditionalists throughout the *Bel Paese*.

Simply put, the period spanning the careers of Coppi and Bartali, roughly 1936 to 1955, represents the first golden age of the bicycle and of bicycle racing. Bike ownership, the era's great symbol of social mobility, was now commonplace throughout 'wealthy' Northern Europe. In post war Italy, beset as it was by a grinding, remorseless poverty unthinkable even in devastated France, the bike came to represent escape, literal and metaphorical, with the enormous practical and social value of ownership possibly outweighed by the spiritual.

Vittorio De Sica's extraordinary 1947 film, *Bicycle Thieves,* perfectly illustrates the importance of the bike as both 'status symbol' and metaphor. Shot amidst the slums and alleys of Rome, the film tells the story of Antonio Ricci, a desperate, unemployed father who finds a job delivering cinema posters, pawning the family linen to buy the requisite bike, which is then crushingly stolen. Too poor to buy another, he and his son take to the streets in an impossible search for his bike. The theft of the machine is highly allegorical, seen to represent an insidious moral bankruptcy, its owner denied the ability not only to work, but to dream. De Sica's Oscar-winning film is today regarded as a neo-realist masterpiece, full of poetic imagery and beautifully understated performances. The symbolism though is extremely powerful; theft is theft, but the theft of the bicycle is truly shocking in that it denudes Antonio as provider and father and this, in turn, damages and diminishes society as a whole. To steal a man's *bicycle* is to steal a man's dreams.

In post war Europe bicycle races – admission free, just stand at the roadside – were plentiful, exciting and dynamic. Italy had her Coppi and her Bartali, while all of France was spellbound by the antics of the neurotic, courageous Breton, Louison Bobet, three times winner of the Tour de France. Cycling obsessed Belgium, home of the brutally fast, inhumanely long, early-season one day Classic races, revered her warriors – hard men like Briek Schotte, Rik Van Steenbergen and Archiel Buysse. Even tiny Switzerland, in cycling terms hitherto a minnow, could proudly boast brilliant champions in 'the two K's', the beautiful, serene Hugo Koblet, known as the 'Peddler of Charm' and his alter-ego the volatile, irascible Ferdi Kubler – Tour de France winners both in the early 1950s.

To place this into context, during my research for this book, I was shown the front pages for Monday 11th June 1951 of both *Tutto Sport*, the daily sports newspaper of Turin, and its Milanese counterpart, *La Gazzetta dello Sport* – owner, benefactor and sponsor of the Giro d'Italia. The race, won by Fiorenzo Magni, the legendary 'third man' of the era, utterly dominated both papers. AC Milan's last day capture of Lo Scudetto, the Italian football championship, provided a significant footnote, but a footnote all the same, to the main event of the day. Bike racing, today beset by weak leadership, a seemingly endless succession of doping scandals, increasingly marginalised even in its traditional heartlands, was then indisputably the pre-eminent sport in mainland Europe.

Researching the great champions who preceded Franco Balmamion then was as easy as riding a bike. Googling 'Fausto Coppi' had revealed the small matter of 329,000 sites with which to conjure, 'Gino Bartali' a little over 150,000. Even 'Magni', his exploits largely forgotten outside his home land, yielded a mind boggling 66,000 options. Repeating the exercise with 'Franco Balmamion' precisely 693 alternatives presented themselves, not one of which contained anything much beyond a set of statistics and the most rudimentary analysis of his exceptional career. Strange, indeed, when one considers that Balmamion not only won two Giri but finished in the top ten on no fewer than five further occasions. In 1967 he was robbed of a third Giro victory by an odious coalition of team-leaders and managers intent not on the glory of sport but on engineering for themselves the most lucrative, politically expedient outcome. He also finished on the podium at the Tour de France, brilliantly won the Italian National Championship and captured several prestigious single day races.

Franco Balmamion was very obviously an extraordinarily good cyclist, one of the very best of his generation. And yet to all intents and purposes lost to the world. Time to find out why. Time to find Franco Balmamion.

STRANGE MEETINGS

And so, here in the lobby of the charming Hotel Victoria, directly opposite the sadly defunct Solo Toro, we wait for 'a man with a black Alfa Romeo, who will arrive at 9 o'clock.' When pressed for a name, Mecu had resignedly, not unreasonably, answered thus: 'Herbie, how many years we are friends? Everything is arranged. Is a friend of a friend of mine, and of Balmamion. Is a Toro fan! You will drive to Savigliano. There will be an amateur race and you will meet there Balmamion. *Is a Toro fan!'*

What Mecu meant of course, and of course he knew I knew this, was that he didn't actually *know* the man's name. He's never been big on semantics.

The phrase 'Is a Toro fan' is more significant than it might first appear. When used by a Torinese it infers that the subject is *genuine* Piedmontese and this, apparently, is very important. During the 'economic boom' of the 1960s tens of thousands of Southern Italians were recruited to the region to work for FIAT. Whilst undeniably beneficial economically this mass migration carried in its wake an inevitable social discord, which still festers at the margins of Torinese society today. One often has the feeling that the Piedmontese still feel themselves put upon even to this day, backed into a corner by the all-consuming, pernicious monster that is FIAT.

At 9 o'clock the Alfa arrives, disgorging the urbane, strikingly handsome Umberto Vai and his endlessly patient, genuinely lovely chatterbox wife, Elida. What ensues is best described as a kind of four-way conversational Snakes and Ladders. Neither Umberto nor Elida speak any English, whilst my wife speaks Italian eloquently and beautifully. Sadly though, only ten words: 'Io non capito, mi dispiace, sono Inglese, dove il gabinetto? (I don't understand, I'm sorry, I'm English, where is the latrine?). This, whilst invaluable in almost any social context, is no firm basis for a fruitful cross-cultural exchange, and so I am obliged to interpret. Which I do – appallingly badly. A little bit of knowledge, you see, is a dangerous thing, and as such I am therefore able to ask all the right questions but not necessarily to understand all of the answers. Still, over the course of an enjoyable, farcical hour or so we somehow muddle along. Sort of.

Umberto seems at pains to point out that his good friend Balmamion is an excellent person with a heart of gold, but that I shouldn't harbour any great expectation that our meeting will be particularly fruitful. He tells me Balmamion is an archetypal Piedmontese: modest, shy and a little detached. He tells me that Balmamion, who in the normal course of events never talks to journalists, has become known as 'The Silent Champion' for precisely that reason. He points out that were it not for the fact that I'm English we wouldn't be doing this today; he tells me that Balmamion had been intrigued that, of all people, an Englishman had expressed an interest. But didn't I ought to be off somewhere playing cricket or Morris dancing?

With the *entente cordial* firmly established we find ourselves parked up and take a short stroll to the Palazzo Royale in Savigliano. To the proletariat it's an impressive masterpiece of Baroque formalist architecture; to the House of Savoy, Piedmont's onerous Royal Family, little more than a weekend hunting Lodge, one of literally dozens dotted here and there throughout the Po valley. It's a classic Italian Sunday morning scene. There are a dozen or so retired though not elderly couples, immaculately, effortlessly turned out, comfortably and enthusiastically meeting and greeting in the early autumn sunshine, in the way that old friends do in this part of the world. And one clumsy-looking, oafish Lincolnshire potato head. Over the years I've come to accept that, the harder I try to look 'elegant' (whatever that means) the more my quintessential Englishness reveals itself in these European situations. For, as an associate of mine is apt to point out, you can't, ultimately, polish a turd. For almost as long as I can remember, my clothes have simply never fitted. Still, my inept sartorial bumbling has its advantages: it's immediately obvious to all and sundry that I am the 'Giornalista Inglese'. Albeit with no shorthand. And a faulty tape recorder. And negligible Italian.

Formalities duly observed, it's to business as the women settle in for a good old-fashioned mothers call and response and the husbands – they're all here (the playground prankster, sage, social conscience, comedian, storyteller, natural born worrier) eagerly convene to smoke, recount oft told stories and, most importantly, *fundamentally*, to inspect bicycles. And for Northern Italian males brought up on Coppi (rider of the legendary celestial blue Bianchi frame) and Bartali (sumptuously rich olive green Legnano – the holy grail for serious race bike connoisseurs the world over) inspecting bicycles, talking of bicycles, of cyclists and cycling is a worthy, serious business. For these people cycling matters not in the humdrum way that politics matters to the politically minded, nor in the casual way that family, friendship, health and happiness matter to the poor lost souls who don't have cycling to define and inform, to control everything they do. Cycling is more than a way of life, more than what people refer to these days as a 'lifestyle'. Cycling is much more important. Cycling is, quite simply, who they are.

One can't help suspecting that this is an unusual finish for a bike race. There are no spectators save for this group of old geezers, no race marshals, no finishing line, almost no neurotic Italian fidgeting. And yet there are bikes, good ones, immaculate ones, lots of them, propped against cars, in boots, on roof racks. Presently a thirty strong peloton, the average age of which I deduce is about seventy, average speed negligible, gently meanders into view, gliding to a halt without so much as a hint at competition. Mecu it seems has for once been misinformed, this is no amateur bike race, but a twenty mile Sunday morning 'bimble' in the country.

Unusually though for a 'bimble', the peloton contains an Olympic gold medallist, a grand tour winner, a World and Olympic Champion and several more notable former professional riders. For this is the regular meeting of the Associazione Piemontesi Corridori Ciclisti, a veritable who's who of former professional riders, and as such Nirvana for a cycling 'historian' like me. So we have the legendary Angelo Conterno, first Italian winner of the Vuelta a España, outstanding roadmen in Mario Vigna and Walter Martin and an authentic Italian track-cycling icon, the stupendously powerful five-kilometre pursuiter, Guido Messina. Sicilian by birth, Messina's talent was so prodigious that in 1948 the technical director of the Italian cycling federation saw fit to forge his identity card, enabling him to win, underage at only seventeen, the amateur World Championship in Amsterdam. He would go on to win the professional version on four occasions, most famously destroying the 'unbeatable' Hugo Koblet in Cologne to claim the 1954 title. During a glittering career, which included Olympic gold in Helsinki and six Italian national titles, Messina supplemented his moderate track income (track riders have always been perceived as cycling's underclass) by riding the professional road circuit in the summer. He won the opening stage to claim the *maglia rosa* at the 1955 Giro in Turin, his adoptive home town.

Finally, joy of joys, there is the almost truly great Italo Zilioli, former leader of the Tour de France and widely considered the best Italian never to have won the Giro. Zilioli finished second at three consecutive Giri between 1964 and 1966 without spending a single day in the leader's pink jersey, the *maglia rosa*. Wiry and fretful and clearly revered by the 'crowd', Zilioli has the look of a man still haunted by what might have been. There's an extraordinary moment as someone spots him rolling in towards the back of the pack. 'Zilioli!, Zilioli!', and he's gasping it, such is the visceral thrill of being here, here at the roadside once more, whilst the eternal bridesmaid, a Piedmontese cycling Jimmy White, acknowledges his supporters, the *tifosi*. For these are the people who suffered through his titanic, though ultimately futile, duel with the great Jacques Anquetil in 1964. They wept for him then, and again in 1969 when, with the *maglia rosa* within touching distance, he cracked on a hideously tough 21st stage through the Dolomite mountains, having heroically attacked race-leader Gimondi on the fearsome Gardena mountain pass.

And then, on foot and almost unnoticed (he's not riding today), a grey haired, compact, sturdy looking sixty-something ambles a little bandy legged towards us. Though I've only ever seen photographs of Franco Balmamion taken over 40 years ago, he is instantly recognisable.

During his racing career Balmamion was often referred to as 'The Chinaman' on account of his slightly narrowed, slightly feral eyes and heavy black eyebrows. Though narrowed further by the bright sunlight and by his advancing years, the eyes, surprisingly inquisitive and sociable, are unmistakably his. Beyond the eyes he has something of the appearance of a country person come reluctantly to the city for an unwanted, unavoidable engagement with stuffy officialdom. The navy pinstriped suit and overly polished black shoes he's wearing, or enduring, are immaculate, uncomfortable and sober. Balmamion has the look of what he is and what he's been – a man born into, fashioned by and delivered from hardship, dues paid up front and in full. He looks in fact like a 65-year-old ex-cyclist, which is to say he looks like a 73-year-old man with nothing more to prove. The Silent Champion arrives, and all seems well in old Piedmont. For, whilst Zilioli, Conterno *et al* are the recipients and beneficiaries of enormous admiration amongst this 'Gruppo Torinese', the appearance of Franco Balmamion, twice a winner of the Giro in the days when the race was the highlight of the Italian calendar, seems to engender a very real warmth of feeling seldom made manifest amongst normally taciturn Piedmontese males. Though they obviously get together often, they're almost falling over themselves to get close, ribbing him mercilessly about his important appointment with the English 'press'.

Franco Balmamion 2006

And immediately I feel apprehensive, mawkish. Never before having interviewed a silent champion in a language I can neither really speak nor understand, I'm suddenly, overwhelming aware that there's a strong probability that the whole episode may well descend into an embarrassing pantomime. Balmamion, though evidently a shy man himself, has agreed to talk principally because he knows I'm not a 'real' journalist, and the synopsis I offer as the basis for our interview seems to put him at reasonable ease, presumably because no credible journalist would ask such facile, dumb questions. He tells me he's happy to tell his story, though first we must eat well. Obviously. It's imperative that one eats well in Italy. Italians love eating well. They're forever eating well, and as a guest in Italy one is obliged to eat well, which is to say copiously, with no regard for anything other than the sensual pleasure of eating. The notion that Italians are healthy because they eat barrow-loads of tomatoes and olive oil is a fallacy. Battered artichokes anyone? Or a nice raw slab of pig fat? And yet it's true – you seldom see fat Italians. They don't as a rule of thumb work hard, for work is, by common consent, rubbish. They don't visit gymnasia (there are hardly any), though they do on occasion stride purposefully to the Gelateria in order to consume annually their own weight in ice cream. Perhaps then it's the prodigious consumption of caffeine and nicotine that enables Italians to exude such good health.

After eating well for seven courses and the best part of three hours, we reconvene to a private members' club where we are joined by Laura Vai, daughter of Umberto and Elida. Laura, who is both delightful and fluent in English, has been drafted in at the last minute to help with the interview lest it hits the skids, though the excellent Barolo we have enjoyed appears to have improved my Italian immeasurably. Then again...

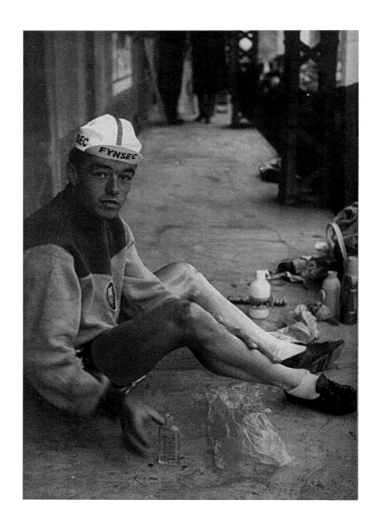

'I WANTED TO BE A CYCLIST'

In January 1940 Giovanna Balmamion gave birth to her second child, a son named Franco, in the tiny village of Nole Canavese, some 25 kilometres north of Turin in the Lanzo valley. In common with all boys born in the valley, Franco's twin birthrights were poverty and a strong cycling heritage. He lost his father, a fire officer, during the Allies' bombing of Turin which saw the fall of Fascism in October 1943, and he and sister Michelina, three years his senior, were raised by their mother. Help came from his paternal uncles, Francesco and Ettore, former cyclists both. Ettore had twice completed the Giro d'Italia (he was fifth in 1931, the year the *maglia rosa* was introduced) during the great pioneering days of Italian cycling. He had himself been inspired by the exploits of the legendary Giovanni Brunero, resident of San Maurizio, some eight kilometres south of Nole. Brunero, famously shy and famously hard, won three Giri in the early twenties, whilst Giuseppe Enrici, from Cirie, sandwiched between Nole and San Maurizio, won in 1924. That these three small villages, within a 10-mile radius and with a combined population of less than 15,000 should produce three unrelated Giro winners seems miraculous, probably without parallel in sporting history.

Young Franco was an industrious, good natured, somewhat reticent child who idolised the Grande Torino and Gino Bartali. Times, though, were desperately hard and there was no way of affording such luxuries as bicycles. Necessity being the mother of invention, the money was somehow found and Franco, aged 17, acquired a bike – initially to get to work at FIAT, in the heart of Turin. He enjoyed the riding and, encouraged by his uncles, joined the local cycling club. Here he found himself under the patronage of another outstanding ex-professional, Secondo Martinetto, a man good enough to have finished fourth behind Enrici at the 1924 Giro. Martinetto, a hard man and a hard trainer, knew precisely what it took to become a *campione della corsa* – champion of the road. What it took, still takes, was principally hard graft and a masochistic predisposition to what cyclists simply term 'suffering' – long, hurtful miles on the bike, day in, day out, rain or shine. Balmamion was pretty good at suffering and quickly fell in love with racing but, though strong physically and psychologically, found himself with an elemental problem – he lacked the speed to win bike races.

Undermined by this deficiency he won only once in his first two years, though he amassed an impressive haul of near misses. This is an astonishing fact in the light of what was to follow. Cyclists of the calibre of Franco Balmamion simply don't not win immediately, or at least pretty smartly after they start racing. To draw a sporting parallel, imagine if you will, an eager, scrawny 18-year-old long-distance runner routinely and regularly losing in regional inter-club races. Now imagine the same athlete only four years later winning the London Marathon. You can't imagine it simply because it's almost inconceivable that it might happen. And yet Franco Balmamion *did* win the cycling equivalent of the London Marathon (albeit a three-week stage race is, in preparation and execution, greatly more demanding than a one-day marathon run) aged only twenty-two.

Progress of sorts was made in 1959. Balmamion, now firmly established at FIAT's spares division, trained hard through the winter and was offered a place with the company's prestigious junior team, the Gruppo Sportivo FIAT. Cycling being what it is, rest forms a crucial part of race preparation (hence the oft-repeated mantra amongst professional riders: 'Never run when you can walk; never walk when you can stand; never stand when you can sit; never sit when you can lie down; never wake when you can sleep'). So Franco was given leave to 'work' directly under Uncle Ettore, and then later, in the offices of the factory for Doctor Cavaglia, himself a cycling fan. Cavaglia's role was essentially to keep him off his feet during work hours, and to facilitate a training programme designed to increase his rapidly developing endurance. They reasoned that, whilst Balmamion would never possess the pure speed to win on flat courses, where the peloton quite often stays together and the sprinters tend to prevail, he could climb well enough to be a contender in the longer, more mountainous races where strength, courage and tactical awareness, rather than straight line speed, are often the deciding factors.

Balmamion won only three times in 1959, but his impressive victory over 145 kilometres at the important Trofeo Garda race in June confirmed him as one of the stronger 19-year-olds in Piedmont – back then one of the great bulwarks of Italian cycling alongside Lombardy, Tuscany and the Veneto. He climbed tidily, albeit without the devastating change of pace which characterizes the truly exceptional *scalatore*, knew very well how to suffer, and could already read a race. But, as the season drew to a close, there was no suggestion that this rough hewn, chronically shy country boy possessed sufficient ability to become anything more than an outstanding amateur rider. Whilst Franco's improved performances were notable within the Piedmontese cycling community, there were, in post Coppi/Bartali Italy, dozens of similarly gifted teenagers in Milan, Florence and Verona. As he approached his twentieth birthday, the last he would enjoy as a junior racing cyclist, time was running out for Franco Balmamion.

So he 'just trained longer and harder, often alone, sometimes behind Ettore's moped, which was quite hard. On the valley roads, or up into the hills if the weather permitted. Thousands of kilometres that winter. I wanted to be a cyclist.' This is a characteristic Piedmontese (and, as I would learn, Balmamion) understatement. For 'hills' read alpine climbs, and 150-kilometres of motor pacing behind a quickening moped is not 'quite hard' at all. It's hour after hour of savagely, unthinkably hard, both physically and mentally. Just ask a professional cyclist.

The training worked. On 20th March, with Italian cycling still in shock following Coppi's death two months earlier from undiagnosed Malaria, a fitter, better, stronger Franco Balmamion won his first race of the 1960 season. He won again the following week and was successful throughout April and May, earning selection for the Coppa Val Maira race in July. The Coppa Val Maira – long and strenuous over 180 undulating kilometres – represented the final chance for Piedmont's better youngsters to earn selection for the Trofeo San Pellegrino, the 'Baby Giro d'Italia'. This mini stage-race held in late September would determine who amongst the elite amateur riders would enter the professional ranks the following season. The 1960 edition of the Val Maira was no contest. Balmamion, stronger and more confident than ever before, attacked repeatedly, demolishing the elite of Piedmontese junior cycling in a devastating show of force. The door to a career in cycling was finally ajar. A good showing in the San Pellegrino might, just might, see him kick it open.

THE SHOULDERS OF GIANTS

Before the Coppi/Bartali era all but the very best cyclists had subsisted in pretty abject penury by today's standards. They rode ridiculous, inhuman distances from March to October, and were by and large fed, watered and feted for their suffering. Though poorly paid, the better riders could at least be reasonably certain of continuous employment for a number of years, assuming that year on year they remained capable of the Herculean efforts required of them by their sponsors and public alike. Coppi and Bartali, and the spell their rivalry cast over Italy, changed all that. With the sporting public generally disinterested in anything much beyond cycling, football, boxing and to a lesser degree motor sport, Italy's three daily sports papers focussed almost exclusively on bike racing during the long summer months, football's off-season. Now the best cyclists were huge, well paid stars, the minutiae of their public and private lives pored over by a rapacious public. The Italian peloton consisted of no more than 120 riders, many of them household names, the fine detail of their exploits an intrinsic element of the fabric of daily life.

They competed across the full breadth of cycling disciplines: single day classics, stage races and grand tours, the winter six-day track circuit, even on occasion cyclo-cross. They made no particular distinction between the various codes; as professional athletes they simply rode every day to win and to earn. They seldom ventured overseas to ride, but competed throughout their homeland to satisfy the voracious appetite for cycle sport. Bartali's extraordinary achievement in winning the 1938 Tour de France is legendary on a sporting level, but also because the notion that an *Italian* might conceive and accomplish such a feat was so utterly quixotic, almost mystical. He wouldn't return to the Tour for ten years, confirming his iconic status by winning again at the age of 34.

Coppi's career from 1939 to 1959, spanning 19 seasons (two were lost as he was in a PoW camp), saw him ride the Tour only three times (he too won twice), while he completed the single day semi-classic Tour of Piedmont on no fewer than 11 occasions. For all its prestige the Tour was of no commercial interest to Bianchi, the cycle manufacturer sponsor of the *Campionissimo*. Cycling teams exist almost exclusively to promote their sponsors, who effectively rent the team owners, riders, bikes, support staff and ancillary equipment for a predetermined period. Cyclists are essentially human billboards, and Italian bike manufacturers didn't generally export their products before the Treaty of Rome saw the establishment of the single European market in 1957.

When Bartali defeated Coppi at the titanic Giro of 1946 the entire peloton was Italian. The following year the Ligurian champion racer-turned-bike-manufacturer, Giuseppe Olmo, broke with tradition and hired a foreigner, the great Sylvère Maes, for the Giro. Maes, twice a winner of the Tour de France, was the outstanding Belgian of his era. The problem was that his era had ended with the outbreak of the war in 1939. In May 1947 he was approaching 38, his best years well behind him. Notwithstanding his publicity value to the cynical, hard-nosed Olmo, Maes was a shadow of his former self, reduced like millions of others to whoring himself around Europe, his only tool a bike, in a sad parody of his outstanding talent. Coppi won that Giro with an epic ride in the Dolomite Mountains. On stage sixteen he attacked and dropped the *maglia rosa* Bartali on the mythical Passo Pordoi, then danced up the brutish Falzarego to claim the second of his five Giro victories. Poor, valiant Maes, out of time and out of his depth, finished the race 15 minutes in arrears.

The genius Koblet's humiliation of Bartali and Magni (Coppi fell and triple-fractured his pelvis early in the race) to become the first foreign winner of the Giro in 1950 left Italian cycling beguiled and bewildered by the Swiss' exemplary talent, so perfunctory was his performance. Though chastened by the ease of it all, Italians at least found solace in the prestige his presence bestowed upon their national tour. What's more, for the first time an entire team of foreigners accepted an invitation to the Giro as Helyett, a successful French bike manufacturer from the Loire, showcased its creations to a quizzical Italian public. Koblet's shock win, and the new money sloshing around cycling, paved the way for other foreign teams to try their hand at the *corsa rosa*. They reasoned that if the Swiss Koblet could win it, anyone could. Couldn't they? Thus began the internationalization of cycling, and of the Giro.

The mid-50s brought the genesis of Italy's 'economic boom' as millions deserted the countryside (70% of the Italian landscape is mountainous or hilly, essentially unsuited to large-scale crop production), and headed for the burgeoning industrial cities, enticed by the seductive neon glow of easy money and the *Dolce Vita*. In 1939 half of the working population had earned a living in the agricultural sector; by 1970 only 17% continued to work the land, so progressive were the new communities, so purposeful the factory floors. This was Italy, the economic basket case of Europe, reinvented; a nation of peasant farmers systematically demobbed, uprooted to shiny new tenements, scrubbed clean and sent out to play, pockets bulging. A tidal wave of optimism and sweet, intoxicating consumerism.

Prior to 1954 professional cycling teams were sponsored solely by a hard core band of bike, tyre and cycle component manufacturers. The races and the racers they supported provided just about the best, in some cases the only, marketing opportunity available in a large, backward country like Italy. At the beginning of the 1954 season, the almost completely bald Magni, erstwhile leader of the Ganna tyres team and quite possibly the hardest, gnarliest, bravest cyclist of his generation, a man with a seemingly limitless capacity to absorb pain, signed a contract with – of all people – Nivea, the face cream manufacturer. Bizarre it may have been, but it evidently did wonders for brand awareness – Magni won a bucket-load of races and in so doing ushered in a wave of *extra sportive* sponsorship deals. Suddenly there were dozens of new teams, often owned by shady entrepreneurial sorts, promoting beer, toothpaste, coffee, fags – you name it. They would be assembled in some instances for one season only, on occasions knocked together for a single race, as a new breed of itinerant cyclist emerged, hundreds of them, schlepping around Europe, anywhere for a ride. Now races, sponsors and riders proliferated further still. In this feeding frenzy many of the new races came and went simply for lack of enough high quality racers, but cycling's popularity seemed infinite and boundless. On any given weekend there were handfuls of races spread throughout the continent, each desperate to attract the stars of the peloton.

The first great race of the cycling year is Milan–San Remo, now held on the third Saturday of March*. *La Primavera* (the Springtime), as it's known, rolls through the flatlands of Lombardia for 180 kilometres, turns right at Genoa, then hugs the stunning Ligurian coast for a further 110 kilometres before climaxing close to the French border on San Remo's most elegant boulevard, the Via Roma. It's the longest, many believe the most beautiful, of all the great classics – the winner can expect to be in the saddle for over seven hours. Milan–San Remo heralds not only

---

* For many years it was always held on 19th March, St Joseph's Day.

the start of the cycling season proper, but also the arrival of spring. The race, like the Giro, is quintessentially Italian. It's a celebration of the beauty of the *Bel Paese*, an annual festival for the towns and villages through which it passes and a pilgrimage for Italian cycling fans.

In 1954 the Belgian, Van Steenbergen, unthinkably defeated favourites Bartali (four times a winner here), Coppi (three wins) and Loretto Petrucci (two) to rain on Italy's great parade. More depressing still, a moderate Frenchman, Anastasi, finished second. A cycling-mad country silently contemplated its collective navel.

Two months later, just four years on from Koblet and the Helyett experiment, foreigners would make up no less than a third of the Giro peloton. Of the 15 seven-man teams entered in the 1954 Giro no fewer than five were foreign national outfits – Holland, Belgium, Germany, Spain and Switzerland – each of them sporting national colours but sponsored by Italian companies. One of Hugo Koblet's Swiss *domestiques*, the naturalised Italian, Carlo Clerici, was allowed to take over 20 minutes from the home-grown stars on an innocuous looking stage six in Central Italy. The favourites assumed he would succumb in the mountains, something of an oversight in view of the fact that the 1954 Giro d'Italia didn't actually visit the Alps at all. Clerici, tidy if unexceptional, was more than capable of following the right wheels in the Dolomites, ably assisted by Koblet, his deluxe model *gregario*. He won the Giro at a canter by 24 minutes, whilst Koblet finished comfortably second and the Belgians took the team prize. Outraged, the press and public rounded on Coppi – quite unfairly, he had chronic intestinal problems – Magni and the other local favourites for their profligacy, accusing them of shaming the Giro. The subtext was unmistakeable: it was all well and good for these *stranieri* to add colour and glamour to Italy's great races, but categorically not for them to walk away with the prizes.

Clerici's win, hard earned, somewhat fortuitous and ultimately largely ignored, underscored an unpalatable truth for Italy. This was the last Giro that the Coppi, Magni and Bartali triumvirate would contest together as 40-year-old Bartali announced his retirement. The golden light cast by the greatest era in Italian sporting history was dying.

It died a little more when another powerful Belgian, Germain Deryjcke, won the 1955 edition of Milan–San Remo, ahead of two little known Frenchman as foreign riders now occupied *all three* podium places. Furthermore, no fewer than six 'guests' finished in the top ten as Coppi shambled in 63rd. Deryjcke was a supremely polished rider, winner of four of the one day 'Monuments' during a five-year period in which he threatened to usurp the great Rik Van Steenbergen at the top of Belgian cycling. Whilst losing to a rider of Deryjcke's class was in itself excusable, abject capitulation to the extent that two obscure French journeymen were able to hijack the lower steps of the podium was both humiliating for the Italian cycling federation and profoundly depressing for the *tifosi*. They needed to get used to the humiliation. Amazingly, it would be a further 15 years before a home grown rider would again triumph on the Via Roma as Italy's great celebration became a shameful, incurable neurosis. Several Belgians, a Spaniard, a Dutchman, a German, those damned French, even an Englishman would win San Remo as the *Primavera* became the embarrassing Pandora's box of Italian cycling.

Later that Spring the 34-year-old Magni temporarily restored order at the Giro, defeating Coppi, a year his senior, by 13 precious seconds to claim his third and final *maglia rosa* in yet another epic struggle, the last of the golden era. Early in the penultimate stage the youthful race leader, Gastone Nencini, punctured, where upon Magni and Coppi, third and fourth respectively, shamelessly attacked. The two grand masters colluded in agreeing to ride a two-up time trial of 140 kilometres, thereby eliminating Nencini and the second-placed Frenchman, Raphaël Geminiani, before commencing hostilities on the final Dolomite climb. This immense struggle was fought for the highest of stakes. Coppi sought to surpass the legendary Alfredo Binda's record of five giri, whilst Magni recognised that a third win would equal Bartali in the record books, if not in the public's affection. Coppi, much the better climber, took the stage, but the Tuscan clung on desperately to claim the pink jersey and his own slice of cycling immortality. Magni would retire the following year whilst Coppi, now bereft of his greatness, concentrated his efforts on time trialing, track-races and garnering lucrative appearance fees. Sadly, the *Campionissimo* never quite knew when he was beaten.

THE NEW CYCLING

The departure of Coppi, Bartali and Magni created a vacuum at the top of a sport in transition. As Italy fretted on the arrival of a new generation worthy of succeeding her heroes, so the proliferation of races saw cycling, and cyclists, undergo a significant change of character and direction. The winner of the next Giro d'Italia, a little known, outrageously talented climber from, of all places, Luxemburg, one Charly Gaul, was typical of the new strain. Though very capable against the watch, Gaul, with his slight build and unusually fast cadence, was essentially a 'pure' climber. He was unsuited to and uninterested in the flatter single-day races, preferring to concentrate his efforts on the grand tours of France and Italy, and on his home tour – in those days a prestigious five-day event taking in both the Grand Duchy and the Belgium province of Luxemburg. The Luxemburg national championship aside, he never won a single-day race of note and never expressed the slightest interest even in those Classics that were better suited to his climbing skills, such as the Tour of Lombardy and the great Ardennes monument Liège–Bastogne–Liège. Gaul, in common with another prodigiously gifted young climber, the Spaniard Federico Bahamontes, was one of the new breed – a grand tour man. Both would achieve cycling immortality within their chosen *milieu* by winning the Tour de France. Meanwhile, in France, an even more brilliant talent, Jacques Anquetil, concentrated largely on time trials and stage races. For all his extravagant gifts and his five Tour wins, Anquetil's *palmarés* makes for curious, lopsided reading. Aside from his victory at the motor-paced marathon Bordeaux–Paris, the semi-classic Ghent–Wevelgem and at Liège–Bastogne–Liège, he too failed to distinguish himself in the muck and nettles of single-day racing in a career spanning 16 seasons.

In Italy a generation of gifted riders like Nino Defilippis, Luciano Maggini and Guido Carlesi, grown accustomed to feeding off the scraps thrown by Coppi and Bartali, concentrated their efforts on Giro stage-wins and the smaller classic races, the single-day punctuation marks of the domestic season. As the swashbuckling, all-conquering heroes of the post-war decade left the stage, the electricity generated by the great generals and their rivalries diminished. Italy searched for the great standard bearers and personalities to emulate them, but found instead a group of richly talented but ultimately mortal 'specialists', broadly speaking single day racers and stage race contenders.

Gastone Nencini, the chain-smoking winner of the controversial Giro of 1957 (he and Bobet attacked when race leader Gaul attended to a call of nature on stage eighteen), was formidable and charismatic. He was a very good climber and amongst the finest descenders ever to have ridden, but fundamentally a stage racer, no Fausto Coppi, no Gino Bartali. The 'Forli Express', Ercole Baldini, briefly galvanised the sport in twice smashing the World Hour Record as an amateur, then winning both the Giro and World Championship in 1958. His success, though wonderful, proved ephemeral. Baldini, the first of a litany of 'new Coppis', abandoned the 1959 Giro, won spectacularly by Gaul, then performed poorly in finishing sixth as leader of the feeble Italian team at the Tour. By the following year his career seemed in terminal decline. Thought by many to have become too rich too young, Baldini collapsed at the Giro, finishing 41st, over an hour down on Anquetil as the Frenchman annihilated the field in a 68-kilometre time trial to Lake Lecco. Anquetil put fully seven minutes into Charly Gaul, four and a half into Nencini, then held on narrowly in the mountains to defeat the latter by just 28 seconds – his first *maglia rosa*. At the Tour poor, likeable Baldini failed again, an embarrassing 33rd as even his time-trialing skills deserted him, shipping four minutes over 83 kilometres to the Swiss specialist, Rolf Graf. Cartoons of the day cruelly depict a bewildered, overweight Baldini grovelling his way up a mountain, unable to support the strain imposed by all of the gold he's lugging around in the bulging, overflowing pockets of his cycling jersey.

For the want of a great rivalry to replace that of Coppi and Bartali, cycling, particularly Italian cycling, became more egalitarian, more diffuse and fragmented. Many amongst the cycling fraternity believed the sport better for it, but the wider public, grown used to the daily punch and counter punch of two genuine greats with very distinct personalities, started to look elsewhere.

With the wonder years an increasingly distant memory cycling, though still tremendously popular, now vied for top billing with football, then just beginning its inexorable rise to the top of the sporting dominion as television ownership, free time and mobility increased dramatically.

THE YOUNG EAGLE OF CANAVESE

1960 found Italian cycling fans awaiting the second coming and, though only an amateur race, the Trofeo San Pellegrino carried a particular resonance amongst the sporting public. Cycling fans, spoilt during the post war decade by the golden generation, had apparently declared themselves underwhelmed by their immediate successors. Italians love nothing more than a good crisis and, in the eyes of the media at least, the sport was close to meltdown for the lack of a Bartali, a Coppi or even a Fiorenzo Magni. Hysterical nonsense of course (Coppi's legacy – vastly increased participation and interest in cycling – had ensured that Italy was bound to be blessed with a further outstanding crop of riders). But hysterical nonsense, particularly of the sporting variety, sold papers in 1960 just as it does today.

For an expectant public, then, the San Pellegrino brought hope. Hope of the renewal of Italian cycling following Coppi's tragic death in January. Hope that from it would emerge a generation of fresh-faced buccaneers eager to take up the cudgels, to re-enact the great battles of the past, to re-ignite the age-old passion for the sport. Moreover, Bartali's presence as race patron added still more piquancy. Coppi's old adversary would surely have agreed that it was time for a new beginning, a changing of the guard.

Franco Balmamion, little heralded and riding for the combined Piedmont team, rode exceptionally well. He stayed in touch over four long, hot days to lie fourth, 20 seconds behind the leader and overwhelming favourite Vittorio Adorni, with De Rosso and Zancanaro second and third respectively.

On the final, mountainous stage to San Pellegrino Terme a group of nine riders escaped, eliminating Adorni and De Rosso, both of whom missed the break. At the summit of the Presolana climb, some 70 kilometres from the finish, the Venetian Zancanaro was effectively leader on the road, with a 30-second advantage on a group of four that included Balmamion. This group bridged across and with five kilometres remaining the original nine were briefly re-united, before Porteri, from Lombardia, attacked furiously. Balmamion clung on to his wheel, as did Tonoli (Lombardia), whilst Zancanaro, having gone hard in an attempt to derail Franco's challenge, was momentarily unable to respond. Suddenly the young Piedmontese needed to find 20 seconds to win the race, a tallish order in only five kilometres, but far from impossible.

Inexperienced he may have been, but Balmamion, schooled by Uncle Ettore and Martinetto, was anything but naïve. He recognised instinctively that in order for the three to stay away from the chasing group containing Zancanaro he required the cooperation of his fellow fugitives. If they could keep the pace high by each doing their share of the donkey work on the front they had a chance. If, on the other hand, Franco, who suddenly had everything to lose, were to tow the others to the finish in order for them to slug it out in a sprint finish, he would surely lose time with Zancanaro's group frantically trying to close the gap. The problem, as always in these situations, lay in the motivation of the other escapees. Top level bike-racing is a ruthless, unforgiving sport, and no ambitious cyclist in his right mind would freely compromise his chances of a prestigious stage-win in assisting another from an opposing team to win the overall classification. Better to sit on his wheel and let him cook himself on the front, saving as much strength as possible for the sprint. Balmamion, unusually animated, takes up the story:

'I needed them to pull, and they knew it. Porteri, who was stronger than me, immediately agreed to contribute on condition that I didn't contest the sprint. If he worked he would win the stage, and if he won the stage he'd probably get a professional contract. I had to pay Tonoli 5,000 lire. That suited me because I got an 8,000 lire win bonus from Gruppo Sportivo FIAT. We made it. I won the San Pellegrino by eleven seconds, and on the podium the great Bartali presented me with the winner's jersey and a contract offer for his professional team, the Gruppo Sportivo San Pellegrino. I was ecstatic. I was about to become a professional cyclist.'

Though flattered, Balmamion didn't immediately sign with Bartali, but instead waited. He and Uncle Ettore gambled that in the light of Franco's new found status as the hottest property in Italian cycling there would be plenty of offers, and they were right. Among the suitors were the Gazzola team, headed by the devastating climber Charly Gaul, in need of a young, strong *domestique* to help him win a second Tour de France – apparently a dream job for a freshman pro cyclist. The Canavese was having none of this, either. Twenty-year-old Franco Balmamion may have lacked for a good education, but he possessed a very, *very* sharp brain. He reasoned quite rightly that cycling was a tenuous career, and that he ought quickly to make hay. Better to be a moderate team-leader than a good *domestique*, reliant on the form and fortune of others to earn a decent living. He reckoned that he could climb well enough at least to make it as a *gregario* (literally a 'helper' – the altogether more human Italian term for *domestique*), so if things didn't work out as a leader he had a ready made fall-back position.

Franco with Gino Bartali on the San Peligrino podium

He therefore signed a one year contract with the moderate, poorly funded Bianchi factory team on the proviso that, aged just 21, he would immediately take on the role of team-leader for the 1961 Giro d'Italia. This way, venerable old Bianchi, in the doldrums following the loss of the great Coppi, received reasonable media coverage (the raison d'être of all professional cycling teams) for their audacity in engaging a fresh faced novice to lead their assault on the great race. In addition, with a young team they were seen to be investing in the renewal of Italian cycling without paying the kind of exorbitant salaries commanded by the seasoned, established stars of the peloton. Balmamion – decent, modest and self effacing, of humble origin and by extension as hard as nails – was possessed of precisely the character cycling fans appreciated. And, crucially, for a team-leader he was cheap. Moreover, the Bianchi team was astutely managed by Pinella De Grandi, former team-mate to Uncle Ettore and Sports Director to Coppi, and arguably the greatest tactician of his generation. A win-win situation.

In view of the interest from Gazzola, Franco and his uncle managed to negotiate an excellent salary for a neo-pro rider. Bianchi offered 150,000 lire a month, an astronomical amount for a first year professional and, in truth, considerably more than Franco Balmamion was able fully to comprehend. The average blue-collar worker of the day typically received about 50,000, as did the average freshman cyclist. That said, though a mind boggling amount of money to an orphan from the Canavese, the Balmamions knew that 150,000 lire wasn't the salary of a proven, established team-leader. In the light of this, and given the precarious nature of the profession, Franco Balmamion wasn't about to take any chances. He requested, and was granted, a year's unpaid leave from FIAT.

Implausibly then, on 20th May 1961, in his home town of Turin, amidst wild celebrations for the Centenary of the establishment of the Republic (20th May is a Bank Holiday; Turin was the first capital of the Republic), 21-year-old Franco Balmamion of the FIAT spares division, previously the winner of precisely zero professional bicycle races, assumed the position formerly occupied by the late Fausto Coppi, that of leader of the esteemed Bianchi cycling team at the Giro d'Italia.

The opening stage was a 115-kilometre *hors d'oeuvre* through Piedmont, into the Alps, over the mythical Col della Maddalena and back again to finish, fittingly enough, back in Turin, at the celebrated Palazetto dello Sport. One hundred and seventy nervous bike riders rolled out of Turin that morning, the small matter of 4,004 kilometres and three weeks from the Giro's traditional finish in Milan.

At the foot of the Maddalena one of their number, a naïve local kid named Balmamion, riding his first Giro for beleaguered Bianchi, launched a gutsy, foolhardy attack. The heads of the peloton (amongst them previous winners Anquetil, Nencini and Gaul), figuring he'd blow up well before the top, 2,000 metres above sea level, didn't bother to chase. Only he didn't blow; he wanted to see his Mum, standing anxiously close to the summit of the climb – the first and only time her nerves would allow her to see her son race professionally. Balmamion simply carried on, waved to his mother, earned a substantial cash prize for being first man over the top, and was finally chased down by a group of three riders only two kilometres from the finish. At the line he was beaten by a wheel length by the great Spanish sprinter Miguel Poblet, but no matter: Balmamion, riding the first stage of his first Giro, had come within an ace of the *maglia rosa*.

He acquitted himself well during the first ten days until, lying fourth overall and idling towards the back of the bunch, he carelessly missed out when a decisive break split the peloton near Naples. With his team-mates lacking the strength to bridge the gap, Franco lost some 20 minutes on the stage, eventually finishing a highly creditable twentieth on general classification, denied a top ten placing by his own carelessness and by the paucity of his team. It was a salutary, salient lesson. More importantly though, during the final week of the race Balmamion rode strongly in the Dolomites, traditionally the breaking point for rookie Giro riders. Notice was duly served: Balmamion, whilst not yet ready to be considered a potential Giro winner, nevertheless possessed the raw materials required of a credible team-leader. He was competent, if unspectacular, in time trials and, on a good day, was able to live with the better climbers. In and around Nole Canavese Balmamion acquired the status of minor local celebrity. He was christened, in the way of these things, *L'Aquilotto*, the 'Young Eagle of Canavese', a pretence he still regards as embarrassing, risible.

Balmamion enjoyed his new life as a pro cyclist and rode well, though without winning, throughout the remainder of the season. He felt no particular pressure following his qualified success at the Giro, and he enjoyed excellent relations with team-mates who, though generally fairly average, were nonetheless committed and ambitious. Despite a useful third-place finish at the important semi-classic Giro d'Emillia, he still couldn't win bike races, but he felt confident enough to take a second year's unpaid leave from work. He signed again with Bianchi, convinced he could be a genuine protagonist in the 1962 Giro d'Italia. Then the metaphorical wheels came off.

During the autumn of 1961 a deal was struck that absorbed the better riders from Fides – the one-season wonder team of surprise Giro winner Arnaldo Pambianco – into its sister team, wealthy, ambitious Ignis. A refrigerator manufacturing firm from Varese, Ignis was owned by 50-year-old Giovanni Borghi, a rich, lugubrious, sports-mad self-publicist. Fides was simply an offshoot brand. In addition to the local football outfit, a World Champion Welterweight named Duilio Loi and the highly successful Varese basketball team, Borghi had bankrolled an expensively assembled professional cycling team for six years. Somehow though, the big prizes, and in particular the grand tours of France and Italy, had always seemed to elude them before Pambianco's coup. Now Borghi, emboldened by Pambianco's unexpected defeat of Anquetil at the Giro, approached Pinella De Grandi with a huge budget and a simple brief: deliver the most powerful team in world cycling and with it the Giro/Tour double. De Grandi immediately bought himself out of the Bianchi contract and re-opened negotiations with Gastone Nencini, winner of the 1960 Tour de France and a free agent following the expiration of his lucrative one-year contract with Borghi. What's more, Ignis was the team of Ercole Baldini, now aged 28 and in dire need of an upturn in his declining fortunes. With three Giro winners on board, and still more cash to play with, De Grandi sought to strengthen his hand further by incorporating the more able riders from Bianchi. Chief amongst them, in theory at least, was the promising Piedmontese, Franco Balmamion, newly cast in the role of a highly paid *gregario di lusso*.

Borghi's contracting of no less than three potential team-leaders didn't play at all well with the Italian sports media. They accused him, rather disingenuously, of using cycling exclusively to further his own commercial interests, inferring that he cared more for the publicity value his association with cycling afforded him, than for sport itself. Not a little rich when one considers that without Borghi and his like the sport of professional cycling wouldn't and couldn't exist, but the inference was plain – Borghi was becoming too big for his boots. Angered and hurt, but anything but stupid, Borghi made great play of removing the Ignis branding from the team jerseys and cleverly re-named his uberteam *Moschettieri* – 'Musketeers', in reference to Pambianco, Nencini and Baldini, the three superstars of Italian cycling. In truth though, the lack of a brand name on the jerseys mattered not; Borghi's profile in Italy, foreshadowing that of the autocratic Silvio Berlusconi some 30 years later, was such that by the time the Giro came around everybody knew who the Moschettieri were and, more importantly, who was signing the cheques. Moschettieri was Ignis and Ignis was Borghi.

Overnight, Balmamion found both his standing and, more importantly, his chances of winning races, diminished:

'The problem was that Pambianco, Baldini and Nencini were all essentially grand tour riders, with similar characteristics to my own. There was no way I would be allowed to race to win, so I asked De Grandi to annul the contract, and signed instead with Carpano, the Torinese team who were looking for a General Classification rider for the Giro. Carpano, like Ignis, was a very good, very wealthy team, with powerful riders in Nino Defilippis and Angelo Conterno. The difference was that these two were both coming towards the end of their careers, and were mainly one-day specialists, capable of winning individual stages and single day races, but, as I understood it, without any particular aspirations for the overall classification at the Giro. Giacotto, the Manager, believed I could ride a good Giro and agreed to match the salary I'd agreed with Bianchi [a stupefying 400,000 lire per month] so I was in.'

Vincenzo Giacotto, the alchemist of Carpano,
in conversation with Fausto Coppi

A CYCLING VISIONARY

Vincenzo Giacotto was a charming, charismatic, street-wise Torinese PR professional. Born in 1923 and raised in Turin's slums, Giacotto found himself orphaned as a small child when his father succumbed to a heart complaint. Unable to support Vincenzo and two older brothers, Signora Giacotto was forced to find work in a textile factory in Turkey, where a skills shortage ensured reasonable rates of pay for competent seamstresses. Vincenzo was raised by an Aunt, subsisting with monies sent across the Aegean Sea. Though impoverished, young Enzo was no street urchin: he would get ahead whatever it took. Not content with the meagre education available to the poor of Turin he resolved to supplement his literacy skills and to secure a place at Technical College. Aged thirteen Giacotto found work at Turin's great steelworks, studying hard in his spare time. At college he earned a degree in technical design but smartly recognised that the money, the real money, lay elsewhere, specifically in show business. He and his older brother set up *Cine*, a magazine promoting new films. In his early twenties he presented himself to Turin's most important Press agency, SPI, and began mixing with journalists and sportsmen, penning syndicated articles for Italy's flourishing magazine industry. He enjoyed the work, the people and the lifestyle. Giacotto was a garrulous, handsome young man, intuitive and talented. People liked and trusted him, and people will always talk with people they like.

In common with most Piedmontese males Vincenzo Giacotto was mad about football and cycling and, although he'd never ridden a bike in anger, he was well regarded within the cycling community. Like all Italians he was intoxicated with the exploits of Fausto Coppi and in 1956, at the age of 33, decided to gamble all on a new venture, the creation of his own cycling team. He invited Coppi to leave Bianchi, with whom he'd spent virtually his entire career, to form a new racing team. Coppi liked Giacotto a great deal and agreed in principle, assuming sponsorship could be secured. The problem was that Coppi was browbeaten by his oppressive, overweening wife Giulia. She controlled the Campionissimo's business affairs, acutely aware of his massive value to any putative sponsor. Fausto Coppi would not come cheap.

To finance the venture Giacotto turned to one of Piedmont's great industrialists, Attilio Turati, the owner of the Carpano company. Carpano manufactured the renowned 'Punt e Mes' – a *very* fashionable aperitif, more expensive than, and considered superior to, the traditional market leader and local rival Cinzano (which takes it's name from the village to the east of Turin from whence it came). What Giacotto presented Turati with was a revolutionary vision for the sport, based loosely around the model employed by Italy's wealthiest football team, Juventus. Traditionally cycling 'teams' comprised a group of individuals riding in the same coloured jersey. There was little or no strategy beyond ensuring that the leader received sufficient water and a vague notion that as many of the riders as possible ought to finish a race. Giacotto's idea was to produce a team in the true sense – cohesive, multi-talented and tactically astute. He figured that a team packed with riders capable of winning would be more successful, more often, assuming he could keep them all happy – no easy undertaking in the macho, adrenaline-driven world of cycling. He asked Turati for a blank cheque and a free hand to sign not only Coppi, but a core of the very best riders, in exchange for excellent results and, of equal importance, the use of his own publicity expertise. Turati duly obliged and Carpano-Coppi was born.

Giacotto, assisted by his outstanding Sports Director, Ettore Milano, set to. Milano would take care of the technical elements whilst Giacotto and his staff would deal with publicity, logistics and contracts – the nuts and bolts of running a professional business. This would leave the riders unencumbered by peripheral matters, and free to concentrate on winning bike-races, thereby garnering for Carpano the maximum publicity. Giacotto assembled a formidable team of Italian riders – handsomely paid (by cycling standards) – and a second group of Flemish riders, expert in the single-day classics of Northern Europe. All told, the team employed around 25 racers, double the number typically retained by a professional cycling outfit at that time, and each of the very highest calibre. They were billeted in the best hotels, ate excellent food and had the best equipment, a team in every sense. When Carpano took to the start line with a ten-man team, typically at least three were potential winners, for only in winning could Giacotto satisfy Turati's ego and, more importantly, guarantee a return on his considerable investment. The results, and consequently the levels of publicity, were predictably excellent. Turati was duely impressed.

Curiously, when an ageing Coppi parted company with Carpano in 1958, Giacotto insisted that the revamped team wear black and white striped jerseys, mirroring those of his favourite Juventus, newly crowned champions of Italian football. Most of the local riders were Toro fans, indignant that they appeared to be representing 'Juve', their sworn enemies. They were persuaded under duress, but by 1961 the Carpano brand name had become synonymous with Juventus, whilst the majority of Piedmontese stood four-square behind 'their' Torino. Turati therefore felt compelled to launch a second cycling team, ostensibly to promote his chocolate brand Baratti, but in reality to curry favour with an increasingly disenfranchised sporting public. Baratti wore the granata jerseys of Torino FC. Sport, and the politics of sport, has always mattered a great deal in Northern Italy.

Nino Defilippis – Carpano's star

'THE KID'

Nino Defilippis remains an iconic figure in Italian cycling. Arguably the most complete, certainly the most celebrated, postwar rider Turin has produced, Nino was a close friend and training partner to Coppi. Coppi it was who dubbed Nino 'il Cit' – The Kid – when in 1952, having just turned 20, he announced his prodigious talent by becoming the youngest ever leader of the Giro. Defilippis, self-assured, outspoken and charismatic – the very opposite of Franco Balmamion – would enjoy an outstanding career. Able to win on all types of terrain, Nino, twice Italian Champion, was a serial winner of Giro and Tour de France stages and major one-day races, amongst them the Tour of Lombardy, the great Italian monument held in early October to bring the season to its conclusion. Several observers cite his victory in the 1962 national championship as amongst the finest performances ever seen in Italian bike-racing. To all intents and purposes, following the departure of Coppi Nino Defilippis *was* Carpano, the re-formed team built around his considerable talent and ego. The Kid was good, and he knew it.

Defilippis is best known in Britain for a race he didn't win, the 1961 edition of the Tour of Flanders. The Ronde is the great classic race of Flemish-speaking Belgium, another of the five monuments of one-day cycle racing. The race, distinguished by short, savagely steep cobbled climbs, is extremely hard and, at over 250km, extremely long.

Defilippis, an accomplished sprinter, approached the finishing line with the outstanding young Englishman Tom Simpson, the two having broken away from the remainder of the 146-man field. Implausibly, Simpson won the sprint as Defilippis appeared to 'die' in the closing few metres of the race. A rose-tinted, Anglicised legend has emerged around the race, Simpson's first significant win as a professional cyclist. Simpson is believed to have played dead, feigning exhaustion as Nino opened out the sprint for the line. Nino then, certain of his victory, relaxed before hitting the line, enabling the Englishman to steal round him at the last possible moment, claiming a cunning, improbable victory.

However, photographs of the finish show a bewildered looking Nino firmly clutching his break levers as Simpson, still sprinting at ten-

tenths, pips him by half a wheel. Bike races are routinely bought and sold, and a second school of thought has it that Tom simply paid Nino for the win. This is inconceivable given their relative standings at the time (Simpson a highly promising second-year professional; Defilippis an established star, amongst the best paid riders in Europe), and the huge prestige the win would bestow on either racer. With the exception of Magni, who won three times between 1949 and 1951, no Italian had ever won Flanders, not even Coppi, who at one time or another won just about every significant race in the calendar.

I met Nino Defilippis at his very famous, very busy Pasta Restaurant in Grugliasco, on the faceless outskirts of Turin. The place is testament to the glory years of Italian cycling, and to his own brilliance. Huge, evocative monochrome prints of Nino with Coppi, Nino arm in arm with Bobet, Nino proudly celebrating yet another win, Nino with his adoring public... I felt compelled to ask him how he'd contrived to lose to Simpson. The Kid, even at 74 a restless bundle of energy, evidently still struggles to comprehend what went wrong:

'It was farcical, they moved the finishing line! The race finished in Wetteren, near Ghent, and it was really windy that day. I felt super strong and Tom kept imploring me, "Don't attack, don't attack. You'll win the sprint anyway." We did three circuits of the town together, and on the final lap the wind had blown the finishing banner down, so I simply sprinted to where it had been sited, directly in front of the podium, the temporary stand erected for the VIPs. It was a formality, and as far as I was concerned I'd won. However, I hadn't realised there was also a thin white line on the road, and Simpson slipped by! I'd already sat up! I was speechless, incredulous! I'd lost the Tour of Flanders! Afterwards all hell broke loose, protests, official complaints, a near riot – in all my years in cycling I never knew anything like it.'

It's a tale he likes to tell (he's an excellent storyteller), but I suspect he's still slightly irked by it, by his own guilelessness.

The Italian season of 1962 began in the early spring sunshine with the now defunct Tour of Sardinia. The race, a gentle five-day event characterised by short stages designed to blow the collective racing cobwebs from the peloton, was won by the great sprinter, Van Looy, with Defilippis impressive in finishing a close third behind Diego Ronchini. From Sardinia the riders decamped to Milan for the world's oldest surviving race, the prestigious semi-classic Milan–Turin, the first big test of the year and an important staging post for those hoping to perform well at Milan–San Remo. A race of the length and prestige of the Primavera demands a minimum 5,000 kilometres of training to prepare for, followed by several warm-up races. Milan–Turin was in those days attritional, twitchy and very fast, nervous riders seeking the insurance of an early-season win. In recent years the race has shamefully been moved to the fag-end of the season, a warm up for the Tour of Lombardy, marginalised to the point of irrelevance.

With Defilippis in France leading Carpano at Paris–Nice, the week long 'Race to the Sun', Franco Balmamion and the rapid Milanese, Toni Bailetti, assumed team leadership for the day. Balmamion was fit, highly motivated and 'at home' as a quality break of 15 escapees ruptured the peloton over a series of medium length, strength sapping Piedmontese climbs towards the conclusion of the race. Reasoning that he couldn't win a bunch sprint – his old Achilles heel – Balmamion launched his attack on the final ascent to Eremo, a climb he'd ridden hundreds of times in training. In so doing he dropped all but Vittorio Adorni, his old sparring partner from their amateur days. Predictably enough, Adorni was a useful sprinter, on paper at least much the better of the two. As the pair approached a packed Velodrome Balmamion appeared to all intents and purposes sunk, undone once more by his lack of outright speed:

'I needed to do something different, because, though I was stronger, we both knew he was faster than me. As anyone who has ever raced would know, in situations like these there is a split second when you gather yourself, clear your head and re-focus your mind on how you will win the sprint, a natural, though momentary break in concentration. Logically that moment would be as you enter the Velodrome, just before you briefly apply your breaks and turn ninety degrees into a completely changed environment. I attacked him in the underpass at the entrance to the Velodrome, surprised him completely. I got a five metre gap, then gave it everything. Once he'd lost my wheel, he was done. My first win.'

As he relives the denouement – to my mind a small masterpiece of strength, resourcefulness and intelligence – there is, for the first time during our conversation, the merest hint of pride, though not of self-importance. Balmamion is utterly without conceit. He simply won a bike-race.

Balmamion's win in Turin, and subsequent excellent performance in helping Defilippis secure the Italian Road Race Championship at the Tour of Piedmont, created a degree of unrest within Carpano. Balmamion may have been flying, but Defilippis, at only 30 the King of Piedmontese cycling, was not yet ready to abdicate. What's more, he didn't much fancy his heir apparent: he found him diffident and uncommunicative and, though secretly impressed by his strength in the hills, made it plain that he didn't believe him ready to lead Carpano at the Giro. A problem then for manager Giacotto, with the *corsa rosa* fast approaching.

Fausto Coppi and Nino Defilippis at the 1952 Giro

A GIRO FOR CLIMBERS

The early sixties saw the emergence of a nascent tourism industry in Italy as wages, car ownership, free time and social mobility grew. A newly formed government department, the catchily named 'Ministry of Tourism and Show Business'(!), headed by the doleful Alberto Folchi, sought to rejuvenate great swathes of the country fallowed by two separate diasporas.

Before the Great War Italy, particularly the impoverished South, suffered from mass migration to northern Europe and, overwhelmingly, to the United States. Between 1876 and 1914 an estimated fourteen million Italians deserted their homeland. Amongst the worst affected regions of the South was Basilicata, the barren, poverty stricken hinterland evoked in Carlo Levi's seminal novel, *Christ stopped at Eboli*. This 'godless' land, crippled by the internecine feuds of the warring brigand clans (forerunners to the Mafia) and by malaria, saw its male population diminish to such an extent that by 1905 two-thirds of all inhabitants were female. The US Consul in Naples reported that: 'The persons emigrating are from the lowest social and economic classes. 75% are Southern Italian males and almost without exception they are illiterate, unable even to write their names.' By 1911 an estimated 600,000 Italian nationals were resident in New York City alone. Even today, entire deserted villages in the poorer regions of Calabria, Basilicata and Abruzzo can still be acquired for the cost of a five-bedroom detached house in affluent Southern England.

In addition, the post World War II period, the 'boom years', saw the wholesale abandonment of small hamlets and villages throughout the South, but also in Piedmont, Lombardia and the mountainous regions of the North-East – the flotsam and jetsam of the much vaunted economic miracle. Folchi, in consultation with *La Gazzetta dello Sport*, decided that the Giro should provide a mechanism for Italians to 'rediscover' the areas they were fast deserting in the rush to prosperity. Launching the race route on 19th April he announced:

'The Giro would seek out and pay homage to new ideas, new attractions and touristic experiences, to the inexhaustible capacity of our country to offer new sensations in areas not only historically important, but above all panoramic and colourful, for persons from all around the world to enjoy. With this edition we will respect the great Giri of the past, but embrace a spectacular, splendid present. This is our project, this is our destiny.'

Blimey! Had Folchi ever ridden a bicycle over a mud-caked mountain pass, what he might have said was this:

'The race will be long, at 4,180 kilometres the second longest of all time, extremely hilly, and run on crap roads often to the most obscure, inaccessible places imaginable. In light of the fact that the last two editions have been pretty dull affairs we've decided to make the route the most difficult ever conceived, an absolute pig for the riders, utterly inhuman. We're including a record *thirty-five* categorised climbs amounting to a ridiculous 318 kilometres of climbing, more than ever before. Fourteen of these will be on *terra battuta* (beaten earth) unmade roads, so they'll be needing lots of spare tyres – there will be hundreds of punctures. In inclement weather some of the climbs will be virtually unrideable, given that they're not really roads at all, they're glorified mountain tracks. One of these, on the penultimate stage, is 10 kilometres long at an average gradient of 11%. We've managed to include seven mountain top finishes, six more than last year. In addition, on the basis that if Anquetil turns up he'll simply annihilate our boys against the clock and defend drearily and comfortably elsewhere, we've simply removed the time trials from the itinerary. There aren't any. Clever eh? Bloody French. This is a Giro for climbers. Italian ones.'

Anquetil shrugged his shoulders and decided he didn't need to win another Giro anyway; he would focus his attention on emulating Bobet in claiming a third Tour de France. They hadn't reckoned, though, on the great climber, Charly Gaul. ('Gaul? Bugger! Forgot about him. Pay him off. *How* much?')

Diego Ronchini, captain on the road of the Ghigi team, felt they'd played into Gaul's hands: 'He'll win it at a canter. If they've tried to adapt it to suit the Italian riders, they've made a mess of it. It's a big mistake not to have at least one time trial.' Gaul, though at 29 approaching the autumn of his illustrious career, remained the dominant climber of his generation. Moreover, he was leader of the Italian Gazzola team and contractually obliged to ride the Giro. He'd won twice before, and fancied his chances here, as did the entire Press Corps.

Beyond the little Luxembourger and the Pambianco/Nencini/Baldini trident of the Moschettieri there were three obvious candidates for the race.

Most conspicuous of the three was Imerio Massignan of the Legnano team. A lanky, angular climber from Vicenza, Massignan was first spotted and later patronised by fellow 'Vicentino' Tulio Campagnolo, supplier of parts for the Italian peloton. Massignan had proved himself a climber *par excellence*, the best of the new breed. In April 1959 Campagnolo had watched on, spellbound, as Massignan, already 22, impressively won an important amateur race near Bologna. Campagnolo wasted no time in alerting an old friend, Eberado Pavesi, veteran Manager of Legnano. Pavesi, one short of the requisite ten riders for the Giro, pitched Massignan into the race – a wild card for the mountain stages. A whole month into his cycling career, Massignan fearlessly attacked during the first week before finding his climbing legs to finish third on a hilly stage to Vasto, nine days into the race. Thereafter he was sublimely brilliant. On stage 12 he finished fifth into San Marino as Nino Defilippis showcased his climbing talents. Two days later, on the difficult stage to Rovereto, he was pipped in a four-man sprint by Rik Van Looy as Anquetil and Gaul, first and second respectively on GC, each lost time. In the Dolomites Massignan rode beautifully, confounding all known cycling logic to finish fifth on the brutal stage to Bolzano, as Gaul in particular suffered badly.

Charly Gaul's mythical performance on the penultimate stage of the 1959 Giro is writ large in the pantheon of great cycling 'exploits'. Gaul, beginning the stage nearly four minutes in arrears to Anquetil, won alone to claim overall victory at Cormayeur, the ski resort at the foot of Mont Blanc. It remains one of the iconic images of the sport, monochrome and indelible. On the final ascent of the St Bernard mountain we see a wretched, broken Anquetil, bent double, losing a spiteful, interminable war with his bike, drowning in pain. Ten minutes ahead there is little Gaul, the so-called 'Angel of the Mountains', floating serenely up the giant pass in what commentators are apt to refer to as his 'state of grace', the effortless, transcendental climbing bliss of which every cyclist daydreams, but which only the tiniest minority can ever experience. The image of Gaul spinning his way up the great Alpine Cols is, to the cycling fan, as evocative as the Matthews Cup final, Owens at the Berlin Olympics, Bradman in his pomp in 1930.

Gaul was probably the greatest natural climber ever to have raced, the most romantic and romanticised figure in the history of cycling, the most romantic of all sports. It doesn't always do to allow plain facts to obscure the great myths we have built for him. Gaul was in the main sullen and detached, unloved and occasionally reviled by the mortals of the Peloton, many of whom thought him arrogant and aloof. Whilst his victory at Cormayeur was breathtaking, nature had bestowed upon him a genius for climbing, the like of which very few have been blessed with either before or since.

The sands of time and the pervasive legend of Gaul have erased the memory of an even more astonishing ride than his own on that unforgettable day, by a figure significantly less celebrated in cycling lore. Though the bare facts of the stage inform us that Imerio Massignan finished second, a mere 36 seconds behind Gaul, three minutes in advance of the third-placed rider, they convey nothing of the context of the stage, nor of their respective positions in the cycling hierarchy. Massignan's display, over 296 kilometres, nine hours and 32 minutes, in laying waste to riders of the class of Anquetil and Van Looy after twenty days of his Giro debut was, it seems to me, still more noteworthy than that of Gaul. Even Gaul, not renowned for his magnanimity, was moved by Massignan's incredible strength: 'He rode well on every climb. He really made me suffer.'

Massignan had no training to speak of for this task, never having once competed in a bike race of over 170 kilometres. He had no experience of the terrain, no notion as to the severity and debilitating effect of a Giro which logic suggested he had not a hope of completing, let alone animating. That Gaul crossed the finishing line alone was due entirely to the fact that Massignan punctured two kilometres from the finish, and that Gaul reneged on a pre-stage agreement he himself had proffered to the youngster. Gaul had approached an awe-struck Massignan that morning offering a deal: if Massignan would collaborate with him in helping to wrestle the maglia rosa from Anquetil, Gaul, clearly the better sprinter of the two, would forfeit the stage to him. In his effusive praise of Massignan's extraordinary ride that day Gaul neglected to mention that the unknown neo-pro had actually towed him up the last climb, the Petit St Bernard, in exchange for a stage-win ultimately denied to him by an untimely puncture and his own (let's say) forgetfulness. Massignan thus finished the Giro fifth on general classification, deprived of a podium finish by less than the time it took to change a rear wheel.

The following year, as a Tour de France debutant, Massignan not only won the King of the Mountains competition but finished a commendable tenth overall – this in spite of losing over nine minutes in the long time trial to Besançon. Like many specialist climbers he was quite inadequate against the watch. At the 1961 edition he finished fourth overall as Anquetil won a non-event by over 12 minutes. More importantly, he eclipsed Gaul in capturing the climbers' prize for a second year, and finally claimed a stage-win with a terrific ride in the Pyrenees.

Though at six feet unusually tall for a mountain specialist, Massignan's skinny torso (he weighed 67kg.) ensured an exceptional power-to-weight ratio. Notwithstanding his beanpole frame, that Massignan was able to compete at the highest level of cycling was miraculous, disadvantaged as he was by a physical impediment which rendered his choice of career and genuine excellence all the more remarkable: he had one leg longer than the other! So whilst Gaul was the 'Angel of the Mountains', the Spaniard Bahamontes the 'Eagle of Toledo', Nencini the 'Lion of Mugello', poor Imerio Massignan toiled under an altogether less glamorous sobriquet: he was 'Gamba Secca', literally 'withered leg'. Don't laugh, it's all perfectly true.

Massignan declared himself delighted with the parcours: 'I like it a lot, and I'm delighted there are no time trials. I think I can win this Giro.' Nencini, appalled by the route, grudgingly concurred: 'I think it's made for Massignan. If he doesn't win this he'll never win the Giro.'

Another entitled to entertain serious ambitions of overall victory was Massignan's close friend and team-mate Graziano Battistini, from La Spezia on the Ligurian coast. Like Balmamion a former winner of the Trofeo San Pellegrino, Battistini, now aged 26, had developed into a thoroughbred Grand Tour practitioner. As a second-year professional he'd been Italian team manager Alfredo Binda's surprise choice for selection at the 1960 Tour de France. Asked by a bewildered journalist why he'd chosen an inexperienced rider with no real pedigree, Binda explained that he believed Battistini capable of winning the race should Gastone Nencini under-perform:

> 'If he rides as I ask he can help Nencini, and he is capable of stage-wins. He is strong, astute and rides well in the heat. He has the potential to win a grand Tour.'

Encouraged by Binda's endorsement, the handsome, shy Battistini surprised the French by jumping away to a 4-second victory over the lightning-quick World Champion, André Darrigade, on the seventh stage to Angers. Three days later, in the Pyrenees, he led over the giant Col d'Aubisque, then rode superbly in support of Nencini when the favourite, Roger Rivière, put the hammer down. He won even more impressively in the Alps as he and Massignan claimed an emphatic Italian one-two over the great cols of Vars and Izoard. In finishing runner-up overall to Nencini, Battistini fully justified Binda's faith. More importantly still he gave the impression that, given free reign, he was indeed a grand tour winner in the making. Though undone by a crash on the opening stage at the 1961 Giro, Battistini began the 1962 season in fine form. He performed well through the spring, culminating in an excellent showing at the demanding Tour of Romandie, the traditional four-day warm-up for the Giro. Here he confirmed both his class and his position as joint-leader of Legnano for the *corsa rosa*.

The firebrand little Abruzzese revelation, Vito Taccone, the new darling of southern Italy, also fancied his chances. A pure climber in the great tradition, Taccone, four months Balmamion's junior, appeared the man most likely to succeed Charly Gaul as the pre-eminent mountain specialist in world cycling. Taccone had signed professional terms with Atala in 1961 and had sensationally won a stage and the King of the Mountains competition at his first Giro. In so doing he'd earned the nickname the 'Chamois of Abruzzo'. In October, at the Tour of Lombardy, Taccone narrowly and contentiously defeated Massignan to win at Como's velodrome. 30 kilometres from the finish Massignan smashed the peloton on the horrendous 20% gradients of the legendary 'wall' of Sormano, a climb thought too steep for modern cyclists and now sadly removed from the race. Taccone, the best of the rest of the climbers, lost 20 seconds on the ascent, and a further 40 on the run-in towards the town as his legs started to cramp. Unusually for a climber, Imerio Massignan was a gifted descender. With four kilometres remaining Massignan entered one of the many long tunnels on the outskirts of Como, his advantage still the thick end of a minute. By the time he emerged into the early evening sunlight the Venetian found himself in the company of a smiling Vito Taccone. Massignan, who was apparently flying that day, estimates that Taccone must have been travelling at speeds in excess of 100kph to have caught him, and he later learned that Abruzzese had stolen a tow from a press motor-bike in the unlit tunnel. Needless to say Taccone, a noted finisher, won the sprint to claim his first major single-day race.

Though tiny at five feet five, Taccone was prickly, aggressive and confrontational on the bike, uninterested in the tactical foreplay which often characterises stage-racing, still more so in the politics and etiquette of the peloton. Taccone's attitude and world view, individualistic and uncompromising, polarised Italian cycling. Aged only 21 he was already immensely popular amongst Southern Italian fans. For them he symbolised defiance – defiance of a Roman state from which they felt isolated and marginalised, and defiance of the traditional northern domination of sport, commerce and politics. Conversely and unsurprisingly he found few friends within a peloton dominated by northern Italian riders, many of whom thought him crude, immodest and unscrupulous – the Southern stereotype personified. For his part, Vito Taccone enjoyed nothing more than thumbing his nose at cycling's ruling classes. For him, cycle racing was simply a test of brute strength, a class war on wheels in which he cast himself as the warrior supreme.

On 25th April, with the riders honing their form three weeks in advance of the Giro, Taccone laid down his marker at the Tour of Piedmont, leading home a seven-man breakaway that featured both Massignan and Battistini. Now the South awaited his consecration.

And not only the South. Guido Carlesi (nicknamed 'Coppino' – little Coppi – because he bore an uncanny resemblance to the *Campionissimo*), a distant second to Anquetil at the 1961 Tour believed the race to be 'incomplete': 'Gaul, Taccone or Massignan will win. It's been handed to them on a plate.' A mortified Pambianco shared his view: 'It's super tough. There won't be a single deciding day because almost every day is brutal. The favourites? Gaul, Taccone, maybe Battistini.'

Rino Negri, chief cycling reporter of *La Gazzetta*, predictably defended the route:

'It's impossible to please everyone: if we fill it with time trials the climbers complain; too many mountains and the sprinters are unhappy; too flat and the breakaway specialists lose out. The riders have their points of view, but they're not charged with designing the parcours. It's a very difficult job. The truth is that the Giro will be won by a real champion.'

Negri next put the boot into Ercole Baldini, a serial moaner:

'Baldini complains that he is at a disadvantage because there are no time trials. Is this the Baldini who finished eighth at the Sorrento time trial in 1960 or the Baldini who complained that the four we included at the 1959 Giro weren't suited to his 'characteristics'? He'd do well to remember his words. We certainly do. Van Looy says there are too many climbs, but declares that he no longer wants to be regarded as a single day specialist. At first glance the Giro may appear suited to Gaul, Massignan and Taccone, but we make no apologies for that. The climbers are entitled to their chance, but equally Pambianco, Suarez, Carlesi, Ronchini and Nencini are capable of winning, as are a host of others. The great champions – Coppi, Bartali, Bobet – could win on all terrains. Why not the stars of today?'

At Carpano, Giacotto offered Defilippis an olive branch of sorts. Balmamion would be charged with securing a top-ten finish on General Classification, whilst Nino, in tandem with the formidable Antonio Bailetti, would attempt to add to Carpano's impressive collection of stage-wins in a plan he christened his 'twin-barrelled attack'. Defilippis was to 'lose' a slug of time during one of the early stages, and in so doing send a clear message to the dozen or so riders attempting to win the Giro *overall* that he was ruling himself out of contention for the *maglia rosa*. This in turn would allow him the freedom to join in or (in the light of his considerable influence within the peloton's hierarchy) to instigate and organise breakaways throughout the race, on the proviso that the composition of any breakaway group didn't impact on the struggle for general classification. In stage-races, GC riders, those with an interest in achieving a high placing overall, are very seldom given opportunities to escape the peloton during flat stages. Only in the mountains, where the slipstreaming effect is negligible and where the strongest always prevail, do meaningful gaps tend to appear at the front of the race.

Crucially though, neither Balmamion nor Defilippis would be designated 'leader'. The riders of a cycling team are allocated numbers one to eight, nine, or ten, depending on the numerical constitution of the team. Traditionally the leader wears the number one, a demarcation signalling his status at the head of affairs. Therefore, taking the 1962 Giro as a typical example, Pambianco, defending champion and nominal leader of the Moschettieri, wore number one, his team-mates occupying positions 2-10. Taccone, leading Atala was 11, Gaul 41, Adorni of Philco 91, Van Looy of Faema 121 and so on. Ever the diplomat, Giacotto assigned his ten-man team of riders their race numbers alphabetically. Carlo Azzini would wear 21, Toni Bailetti 22, Balmamion 23, Germano Barale 24 and so on, denying Balmamion a kudos for which he cared not one iota. Pedantic nonsense? Possibly so, but Balmamion had yet to earn his spurs on the road, whilst Defilippis remained, by common consent, a *Campione della Corsa* – a Champion of the Road.

Moreover, when Giacotto announced the room list for the opening stage of the Giro, Franco and Nino were surprised to find themselves pitched together. Balmamion's natural inclination would always have been to share with his good friend Toni Bailetti, while Nino had, in the veteran Angelo Conterno, a superb first lieutenant and confidante. Giacotto, blessed as he was with an acute human intelligence, recognized that Balmamion's promising spring campaign had provoked early signs of insecurity in Defilippis. In having the two room together he sought, as was his wont, to head off any potential conflict at source. He understood very well that Balmamion revered Nino and hoped that the Torinese could not only learn to understand the youngster's shyness, but grow to appreciate the deference and humility at its root. If Nino could be persuaded to take him under his considerable wing, Franco might feel emboldened, might even emerge as a genuine contender for a top five position. For his part Nino, resplendent in his National Champion's *maglia tricolore*, would in theory repay the management team's implicit compliment in investing him with the responsibility for taking care of their GC man.

Another pearler from Vincenzo Giacotto's book of very smart moves; Nino agreed to room with Franco for the opening week of the race. Time to get down to business.

Km. 0 ━━ 50 ━━ 100

LE BALCONATE VALDOSTANE
TERME DI ST. VINCENT
APRICA
MOENA - CAVALCATA DEI MONTI PALLIDI
BELLUNO
PIAN DEI RESINELLI
LECCO
MILANO
NEVEGAL
CASALE MON.
LIGNANO SABBIADORO
TABIANO BAGNI
SALSOMAGGIORE
FRABOSA SOPRANA
SESTRI LEVANTE
BAIA DELLE FAVOLE
ALTA VALDINIEVOLE
CASTROCARO TERME
PANICAGLIORA
MONTECATINI TERME
FANO
CITTA' DELLA DOMENICA
PERUGIA
VALLE SANTA
RIETI
VALLE DELLA
RINASCITA
CHIETI
FIUGGI
FOGGIA
MONTEVERGINE
AVELLINO
C. SAN-

organizzazione
La Gazzetta dello Sport

60

PART TWO

THE 1962 GIRO d'ITALIA

Pre-race favourites, Taccone, Gaul and Massignan
shake hands on the start line in Milan

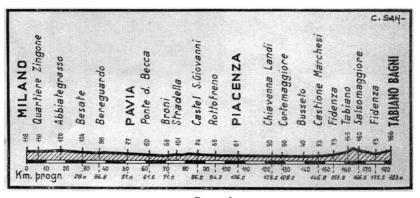

Stage 1

STAGE ONE

On 19th May 1962 the opening stage of the 45th Giro d'Italia – 185 kilometres run off in howling wind and pouring rain – departed Milan's extraordinary gothic cathedral, the finest in all of Europe, for the Spa town of Tabiano Bagni. The race was made by a three-man escape after only eight kilometres, as Taccone's team-mate Franchi, the Spaniard San Emeterio and the breakaway specialist Renato Giusti of Torpado sped away, quickly establishing a five minute advantage on the peloton. Three minnows chancing their arms, Kings for a day leading the Giro (they'd tell their grandkids), glorious victors in the phoniest of phoney wars. Caught by the peloton after 135 kilometres if you must split hairs.

Some 15 kilometres from the finish the old lion, Nencini, fancifully recast as Athos, the sagacious elder statesman of the musketeers, attacked with 20-year-old Guido Neri, a wide-eyed neo-pro mixing it with the big guns, living the dream in his first season amongst the highwaymen of the Giro.

All for one and one for all, Nencini's calculated burst fractured the peloton as a second wave of 21 riders, containing Baldini and Pambianco as well as the Legnano pair, Massignan and Battistini, wriggled free in pursuit. By the time he and Neri were reeled in eight kilometres from the line, the senior Moschettieri's sabre rattling had detached Taccone, Gaul, Defilippis and Balmamion. Finally, in the 23-man, 60kph stampede for the line little known Dino Liviero of Torpado sprinted to the biggest win of his life and to an unlikely *maglia rosa*. The archetypal one-hit wonder, Liviero would fail to win again before retiring from professional cycling in 1964, aged only 26. Six years later he would lose his life, killed by a speeding car as he cycled through an unlit tunnel near his home town of Treviso.

Though Liviero's tyre width coup was both surprising and prestigious, of greater significance was the split which ultimately saw Taccone and Gaul, Defilippis and Balmamion lose 1'38". By no means a disaster for Carpano, but a pretty inauspicious start, to say the least. Not remotely good enough.

Guido Neri

GREGARIO

In a nine-year professional career made remarkable by the fact that at first glance it appears so *unremarkable*, Guido Neri would win just one bike race, at the inaugural Trofeo Laigueglia, the very first event of the 1964 season. If we make the most conservative of guesstimates, based on only 100 competitive rides a year (very small beer in the sixties) that's 899 races he took part in and failed to win – on the face of it a pretty staggering non-strike rate, even for a *gregario* paid not to win, but to assist others in so doing. One victory salute in 900 outings then, the more memorable for it and nothing short of fantastic in the light of the circumstances surrounding the race.

The son of a fruit grower from Cesena in the Communist stronghold of Emilia–Romagna, Neri was a promising junior boxer until a badly damaged septum saw him abandon the ring and try his hand at bike racing, much to the delight of his father, a cycling nut. With the nearest cycling club some thirty kilometres from home, young Guido would begin his training rides with the lung-busting pursuit of a moped ridden by a wealthy friend in order to arrive at clubhouse on time. He started winning races immediately and enjoyed a prolific junior career. With over 50 successes he earned selection for the national team at the 1960 Amateur World Championships, held for the first and only time behind the iron curtain, in East Germany. Sidelined by injury, Neri never made the start line as the Italian team flopped. A local, Bernard Eckstein, confirmed the 'moral, cultural and sporting supremacy of the Eastern bloc' (according to an East German report) by completing a hat-trick of successes following two previous wins by his countryman Täve Schur, later voted East Germany's Sportsman of the Century.

In 1962 Neri signed a one year professional contract with Torpado, the Venetian frame builder. Following a winless, though promising, first season he accepted an invitation from Gino Bartali to join his San Pellegrino team for 1963. When, following a row with the Italian cycling federation, San Pellegrino withdrew from cycling after the Giro, Neri and his team-mates found themselves in the employ of FIRTE, an electrical goods company of dubious virtue. The only problem was that FIRTE, like any number of Johnny-come-lately cycling sponsors down the years, didn't have any money, and as a result Guido Neri's role within the team changed dramatically. Unable to pay much more than half the wages due to him, FIRTE were nevertheless kind enough to offer young Guido the position of delivery boy, an opportunity not only to just about feed his family, but also to improve his driving, installing and lifting-heavy-things skills. These sportsmen don't know they're born. Though handy with a screwdriver, Neri failed for a second consecutive season to win any races and, when FIRTE cut and ran, he found himself out of cycling and unemployed.

The Trofeo Laigueglia, these days an established fixture in the Italian season, was conceived to showcase the charms of the Ligurian coastline to the west of Genoa. Attracted by the warmer weather the Riviera offered, most of the Piedmontese and Lombard teams held early season training camps there anyway, so Laigueglia was an ideal spot for an early season pipe opener. At Masone, a small mountain village of 2,000 inhabitants some 20 minutes inland, the old lags of the *Dopolavoro* (After Work) Social club had a whip round and approached a local cycling agent to knock together a small, reasonably priced team on their behalf – not a particularly difficult task with several riders 'between jobs' and a thriving local scene. Towards the finish of the race, a high-value seven-man group, that included a future world champion in Adorni and a Tour de France runner-up in Carlesi, escaped the peloton. Lo and behold, Guido Neri made the breakaway, evidently having failed so to do throughout the preceding two years. More improbably still, 15 kilometres from the finish Neri, hung for a sheep as for a lamb, attacked again, got a gap, put his head down – and prayed.

Twenty or so minutes later he rode in splendid isolation across the finishing line, out of the last-chance saloon and into a contract offer with the Gruppo Sportivo Molteni, the powerful cycling team of the giant Milanese sausage meat and Salami manufacturer. For three years Neri served as a *gregario* to the great German champion, Rudi Altig, and the beautiful, enigmatic (many said unmanageable) Gianni Motta. Neri, typically selfless, rode solidly as Motta easily won the 1966 Giro, the crowning achievement of a career characterised by tantrums, polemics and the wondrous purity of his pedalling style. In the winter of 1966 Neri, again without a contract, moved north to Milan and began work in his father-in-law's family business, done with cycling. Only he hated the cold and snow of the Milanese winter, the claustrophobia of the big city and the world of work. Finally he called his old mucker

Nencini, Sports Director for the newly formed Max Meyer team, to ask for another chance. With Nencini he spent three good seasons before signing off with SCIC, a kitchen manufacturer, in 1970. In all Neri rode eight Giri and never failed to finish. He never won a stage, never in truth came particularly close to winning one. He never won the King of the Mountains or points prize, neither scandalised nor animated the race. He never complained, never harboured any personal ambitions other than to serve.

Guido Neri's back-of-a-postage stamp sized *palmarés* suggests his crowning glory as a cyclist was the solitary win on the Ligurian coast. It wasn't. In trying to track him down for interview, I asked around a few of his contemporaries for their memories of a rider who, given that his only success was achieved wearing the colours of a pub team, failed to win a single bike race as a professional. To a man they agreed that Neri was an outstanding rider – exceptional in the mountains, brave, unstinting and loyal. They all said he was *simpatico* (loosely translated – generous in spirit), the hallmark of a good *gregario*. Neri, like the great silent majority of professional bike riders, was a grafter, a fetcher and a carrier, no more and no less. And no less a giant of the road for it.

Like hundreds of former cyclists, Guido Neri now owns a bike-shop in his home town, supported, in the best Italian tradition, by his wife and son.

STAGE TWO

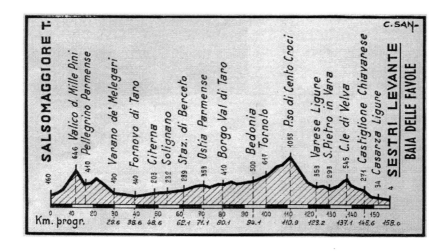

Stage two comprised 158 alternatively cold and wet, then warm and sunny kilometres to the idyllic Ligurian fishing village of Sestri Levante, along the way from the French border. Today saw the first major obstacles of the Giro, as the peloton left wealthy, flat, fertile Emilia-Romagna and crossed the Apennines into the Ligurian hills. Fifty kilometres from the finish, on the 12-kilometre ascent of the Passo Cento, Croci Battistini, keen to establish his credentials as team-leader at Legnano, attacked with such prodigious strength that the peloton immediately splintered. As Battistini powered on ahead, a cohesive chase group of nine formed, driven along by defending champion, Arnaldo Pambianco. With the main bunch behind already in disarray the unfortunate Vito Taccone punctured. Taccone waited furiously alone for over two minutes as his team car struggled through the mayhem in appalling weather conditions. He would lose more than five minutes to Battistini, whilst Gastone Nencini disastrously conceded six. Then, with the remainder of the favourites fighting to bridge across to the Pambianco group, Franco Balmamion's form inexplicably collapsed to such an extent that he lost eight minutes to the main body of the Peloton, ten to Battistini:

'It was a hunger knock. I hadn't eaten enough and simply ran out of fuel. None of the team waited to help me, nor could I expect them to. I hadn't earned their loyalty and had no real pedigree, so I was left to fend for myself. I let Giacotto down and I felt humiliated.'

These were the days of the *Amiraglia*, the single 'Admiral' team car. Each team was allowed only a single support vehicle, manned by a driver, a *Directeur Sportif* and a mechanic, able to provide medical and mechanical assistance but not to carry food. Those who 'bonked' paid heavily. As Battistini held on to secure both stage and *maglia rosa* on his home turf, for the shell-shocked Balmamion, already eleven minutes adrift, all seemed irredeemably lost.

Furthermore, Vincenzo Giacotto was presented with the very worst case scenario. His 'one gun, two bullets' strategy having spectacularly back-fired, he now looked to Defilippis to salvage a high position on General Classification. Whilst he was under no illusion that Nino could actually *win* the Giro (he'd never climbed well enough, often enough to be considered a serious contender for the podium) Giacotto sought to convince him that he, and not young Balmamion, was the man for overall success. Clever, inventive Giacotto persuaded Nino that he'd been right all along about the 'Chinese' Balmamion, and that he should forgo his chances of heroic stage-wins and concentrate fully on fulfilling his destiny, to finally win the Giro d'Italia. He was to add his illustrious name to those of Coppi, Bartali and Magni, to confirm his position amongst the true greats of Italian cycling. The *gregari* would be put to work in his service, leaving Balmamion to feed off whatever breakaway scraps he could muster. Giacotto also believed that in Toni Bailetti, 37-year-old Conterno and the talented Swiss, Kurt Gimmi, his team possessed three riders capable of picking up the odd stage here and there.

Giacotto's appeal to Defilippis' vanity worked perfectly. Plan B then for Carpano.

Graziano Battistini

STAGE THREE

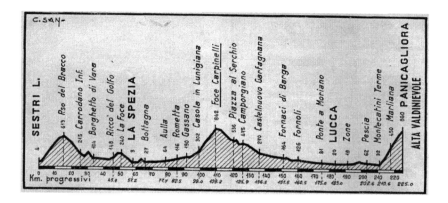

Stage three saw the Giro reach the wild, rugged landscape of the Valdinievole in Northern Tuscany for a mountaintop finish at Montecantini Terme, a tourist trap made famous for the restorative powers of its thermal springs. The official bumph handed out to the hacks of the Giro makes for seriously impressive reading, if perhaps a tiny bit overblown: 'Rich, curative waters offering a range of treatments such as motion therapy (more commonly known, I believe, as '*swimming*') and remedies for tubotympanic insufflations ('*earache*'), intestinal and vaginal irrigation (let's just not go there). Treatments are also available for arthritis, gynaecological disorders and gout.' The Spaniard, José Pérez-Francés simply couldn't wait. Unable to contain his excitement (or perhaps his gout!) Pérez-Francés, normally a model stage-racing professional, embarked on an ambitious, queue-jumping 100-kilometre breakaway, only to be reeled in as the desperados of the peloton fought tooth and nail to beat the rush for the baths. Four of the more hopeless cases (the Dutchman Hoevenaers from Philco, Germano Barale of Carpano and the young Spaniards Galvanin and Salvador) then tried their luck as the peloton, delirious with all manner of urinary, intestinal and colonic insufflations, set off in desperate pursuit. At the historic, sober, fortress town of Lucca, Vito Taccone, the 'Chamois of Abruzzo', jumped away from the chase group, accompanied by Zancanaro and Huub Zilverberg, one of Rik Van Looy's powerful Faema *rouleurs*.

As the pace intensified on the final climb the Spaniard, Angelino Soler, a wonderfully balletic climber from Valencia, changed up a gear and set about reeling in the Taccone group. Only two riders, the Belgian Armand Desmet and a 21-year-old Giro freshman named Vincenzo Meco, were able to keep pace, albeit briefly. The red-headed Meco had grown up alongside Vito Taccone in Avezzano before being plucked from obscurity by Gino Bartali. Taccone, a very big shot in a very small town, hadn't taken at all kindly to his erstwhile friend's elevation to the professional ranks, a fact seized upon by the media as the cold war between the two escalated. Soler, riding for the Italian Pasta maker Ghigi, caught the leaders three kilometres from the top, then attacked again. Nobody, not even Taccone, was able to respond. Soler rode easily away to win by 33 seconds from a four-man group comprised of Taccone, Meco, Desmet and Zilverberg. Five seconds later came Balmamion, Defilippis, Gaul, Guido Carlesi, Baldini and Soler's team-mate, Antonio Suarez, a half-minute in advance of a 21-man peloton containing, amongst others, Pambianco, Battistini and Imerio Massignan. Suarez, third at the 1961 Giro behind Pambianco and Anquetil, thus claimed the leader's jersey from Battistini, whilst Balmamion, solid if unspectacular, at last found a little form and stopped the rot.

Before dinner Charly Gaul modestly explained to Italy's sporting hacks that yes, he had indeed only soft-tapped his way up the final climb, that yes, he did feel in particularly good condition, and that yes, he believed he would win the 1962 Giro d'Italia. Gaul went on to explain that the opening skirmishes mattered little, that Anglade and Desmet had simply been wasting their energy and that the race wouldn't truly begin until the Dolomites. Gaul politely concluded that he hadn't seen anybody he thought capable of threatening him in the mountains, probably not Massignan and certainly not Taccone, whom he believed 'imprudent'.

Notwithstanding Suarez's *maglia rosa* and Soler's inspired dash, the talk of the Giro that night centred not on the Spanish coup, nor on brave Meco's dual with the wilful, obdurate Taccone. Though Defilippis was strong and Baldini apparently resurgent, amongst the sick and the needy, amongst the gynaecologically challenged and the colonically irrigated of Montecantini Terme the word was out. And the word was Gaul.

STAGE FOUR

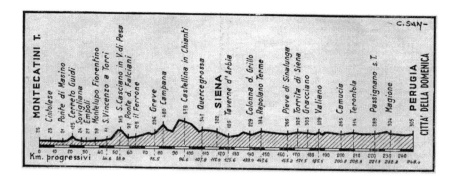

The fourth stage comprised 248 scorching, lumpy kilometres to Umbria's latest tourist hot-spot, the appallingly badly named Citta della Domenica – Sunday City. Sunday city was conceived as a kind of Italian Disneyland, albeit without direct connection to Disney *as such*. It still limps along as a kind of tourist attraction today, having been remodelled as an above-average wildlife sanctuary. Quite what takes place at Sunday City on Mondays, Wednesdays and Thursdays I have no idea, though it's not difficult to suspect that a name change might engender an upturn in business. If you find yourself in Perugia and it's boring (unlikely since downtown Perugia is particularly pleasant, easy paced and lazily interesting), and it's Sunday, it might be worth a look, sort of.

The stage to Sunday City took place on a Tuesday and saw Antonio Bailetti, Carpano's next big thing, escape in the heart of that part of Tuscany latterly known as Chiantishire. Though aged only 22, Bailetti was already right up there in the Carpano hierarchy, licensed by Giacotto and Milano simply to go out and win. Whilst Nino and Franco were unquestionably Carpano's big hopes for the Giro, Toni was so good and so strong that he could win on any given day, rain or shine, short stage or long, hilly or flat. Bailetti could win a bunch sprint, a rolling stage or a time trial. He was Giacotto's wild card, not for him the thankless fetching and carrying of the *gregario*. Young Toni was better than that – much better. At Siena he claimed the day's intermediate sprint, and in so doing earned for himself the not inconsiderable reward of a very nice, very large sheep. Bailetti, as strong as an ox but blessed with much better bike handling capabilities, stayed away to win by over four minutes, precisely as Giacotto had called it.

Back down the road, Balmamion, now ostensibly a GC no-hoper, was quick to follow, though not assist, a counter-attack by his old adversary Zancanaro, now riding for the Philco team. Only when it became clear that Bailetti's lead was unassailable did Balmamion contribute. Zancanaro's strength ultimately saw the pair claw back almost two minutes on the overall race leaders as a disinterested peloton idled across Central Italy. Small change perhaps, but it did wonders for Balmamion's morale. The catastrophe at Sestri Levante and his difficult non-relationship with Defilippis had all but persuaded him to quit. Now, relieved of the burden of expectation, he simply rediscovered the joy of riding his bike. Flushed by his friend Bailetti's success and by his own improving form he felt ready to impose his own will on the race. Never say never.

Antonio Bailetti

THE MAN WHO FELL TO EARTH

Antonio Bailetti rests easy in his tiny home on the outskirts of Milan and talks of a bitter-sweet life in cycling, in particular about the joy and sorrow he felt in winning an Olympic gold medal. He talks animatedly about the day he won gold, about the thrill of winning the blue riband Tour de France stage into Bordeaux and of his stage-wins at the Giro. Bailetti talks of his many failures too, of the puncture which deprived him of the final stage of the 1963 Tour, of the day he very nearly won Milan–San Remo. Approaching his seventieth birthday Toni remains an impressive, distinguished looking man, every inch the Olympic champion he once was. He is unpretentious, affable and intelligent, a willing talker and a pretty good listener. He's a very likeable man indeed, and particularly easy company on this late summer afternoon. Better still, when he talks cycling he's concise and perceptive, as if he has a higher understanding. Only look closer and you'll detect a certain melancholy in his gaze. As he thumbs through the scrapbooks his wife, Ivana, assiduously compiled throughout his career, Toni's eyes are a window on what might have been and wasn't.

Antonio Bailetti was the son of an itinerant farmer from the destitute region of Vicenza, 60 kilometres to the west of Venice. In 1949 the family, like a great many of their neighbours during those atrocious postwar years, migrated further west still, to the prosperous, fertile plains of Lombardia. Toni's father, the oldest of twelve boys, settled in Turbigo, an artless, humdrum commune close to Milan. Here the family began the long, gruelling march to solvency, determined not to get ahead – no such concept existed for the likes of the Bailettis – but simply to put in enough 14-hour shifts to keep the (rented) roof on.

In the summer of 1951 11-year-old Toni left primary school to commence his working life and, as chance would have it, his career as a cyclist. He began delivering bread from 3 a.m. seven days a week, 52 weeks a year. And Toni was a *formidably* good delivery boy, punctual, fastidious and cheerful – the very best in Turbigo. Pelting around the town in the small, dark hours of the morning, young Bailetti made it his business to get the job done in double-quick time. For in the afternoons Toni Bailetti, a sucker for punishment like his Dad, would put in a second long shift of his own, teaching himself how to become a professional cyclist whilst riding a trade-bike. He couldn't wait to get started.

In 1953 Toni's boss reluctantly allowed him to start removing the bread baskets of a Sunday afternoon, to join in with the local racers. The following year, still riding his embarrassing old clunker, he began beating Milan's all-the-gear-no-idea teenagers with their swanky Bianchi racing frames with their Campagnolo and Simplex components. Now who was embarrassed? Aged 16, Toni Bailetti had not only joined the Cademarteri cycling club, but had a real racing cycle to race on, bought for him by his boss. Though the bike was four inches too small for him (Toni was a very big teenager) even that couldn't stop him winning races.

By 1958 Toni was simply riding away from the best Lombardia could offer, so prodigious was his strength. Week in, week out his enormous legs (and I mean enormous – Bailetti has the biggest thighs I've ever seen) routinely propelled him to comfortable, emphatic victory. Success on a bicycle came embarrassingly easy to the young *Turbigese*, a winner in a sport defined by also-rans. Grown tired of beating the same old faces, eighteen year old Toni Bailetti and three of his friends from the club, Cogliati, Fornoni and Forti, hatched an audacious plan – to form an unbeatable four-man time trial team, their sights set firmly on the Olympics to be held in Rome in 1960. Both on and off the bike they became inseparable, concentrating their planning and preparation on earning selection for the 100-kilometre event, the longest and most barbaric of the team disciplines. By the early summer of 1960 they were unstoppable, winning the Northern region final eliminator in record time, despite a strong headwind. In late June they repeated the dose at the National Championship, averaging almost 50kph, a shooin for the Olympics.

Only not quite. In announcing the Olympic team on 13th July 1960 the Technical Commission inexplicably saw fit to omit Forti, at 18 the youngest of the quartet, in favour of Livio Trapé. Why had they changed tack so late in the day?

'It was entirely political. The games were in Rome and Trapé was a Roman. Don't get me wrong: he was a good man and very strong, but certainly not as strong as Forti. We perfectly understood why they did it and it was devastating for Forti, who was completely crushed. He and I were very close and he was already stronger than Fornoni and Cogliati, even at 18. He abandoned cycling when they left him out, pretty well abandoned everything in fact. I tried to help him afterwards and I missed him greatly, but he never recovered at all and just drifted along, his heart really broken.

The week preceding the Olympics was horrendously hot and one of the Danish riders died in the road-race. I never got the official version, but I suspect the heat played a big part, it was so oppressive. It was awful, but we wanted to realize our ambition so we tried to stay focussed on the job. Then we were led to understand that the Russian and East German teams were using drugs and we didn't know anything about those things back then, so we had no idea what we would be up against. The harmony of the group was broken because Trapé was uncomfortable and we felt cheated that our friend wasn't there with us. In the event we won the Gold medal by two minutes, but I'm pretty certain we would have won it by four had Forti ridden. Of course it was fantastic to win, but I can't say I enjoyed the ride itself. The heat was murderous and we were winning the gold while Forti was sat at home. I still feel guilty to this day in fact.'

Gian Piero Forti died unconsoled aged just 60.

His place secured in Olympic history, Toni Bailetti joined, along with Franco Balmamion, as a debutant at Bianchi. He won his very first race, a stage of the 1961 Tour of Sardinia, and adjusted seamlessly to life amongst the professionals. Courted by Vincenzo Giacotto he followed Balmamion to Carpano at the season's end, seemingly destined for greatness. For two years Bailetti won prolifically, most famously at the Tour, first in Rennes and then at Bordeaux's prestigious old velodrome. Three days before the 1962 Milan–San Remo Giacotto called him to Turin for a meeting. Arriving at the Carpano office Toni found waiting a huge phalanx of reporters and photographers. Giacotto, as adroit a psychologist as he was a publicist, had called an 'impromptu' press conference pronouncing Antonio Bailetti the next winner of the Primavera! Though astonished and acutely embarrassed, Toni very nearly pulled it off, pipped by the powerful Belgian Daems, following an outrageous 160-kilometre lone breakaway. No matter, he won often enough to earn selection for the eight-man Italian team at the World Championships, confirming his position as amongst the men most likely. Bailetti was a very bankable commodity, a winner of bike races.

Whilst Bailetti was away beating the best cyclists in the world, a second buccaneering son of Turbigo, one Raffaele Marcoli, was emerging triumphant from the local amateur scene. Marcoli, a sprinting specialist known locally as 'The Arrow', had spent a life in and around bikes helping his father out in the family business, a cycle shop. He and Bailetti would train together through the winter months and Marcoli, desperately clinging to Toni's wheel for mile after excruciating mile, felt the benefit when, in 1963, Legnano offered him a pro contract. Though he couldn't climb, Marcoli's finishing rush was so powerful that on his day he was all but unbeatable in a sprint. In winning a number of Giro stages, Raffaele quickly built for himself a reputation amongst the very best finishers in Europe, occasionally eclipsing Darrigade, Graczyk and Altig, the established greats of the day. Moreover, the natives of dreary Turbigo finally had something to cheer about, their very own (poor man's) Coppi and Bartali.

Bailetti and Marcoli were united professionally in 1966, signing for the same team, Sanson. On 13th August at Lake Maggiore, 26-year-old Marcoli won the Coppa Bernocchi, then one of the big single-day classics on the Italian calendar, an unofficial national championship for sprinters. Thirteen days later the Arrow of Turbigo, the best *velocista* in Italy, took his fiancée and future brother-in-law out for a spin on the very roads he'd ridden to the most important victory of his cycling career, decoding and reordering for posterity the emotional and psychological madhouse that is a bicycle race. There, in the early evening sunshine, Raffaele Marcoli, the great dare-devil of the sprint, took one overtaking risk too many, crashing tragically into an oncoming truck. Lights out in Turbigo.

Toni Bailetti carried on racing, but he's honest enough to admit that his heart wasn't truly in it. Carpano had disbanded and Toni now found himself working principally as a *gregario* for Italo Zilioli and the outstanding sprinter Mino Bariviera. He was reasonably well off, having invested his winnings in a sportswear manufacturing business operated by his wife. Amidst the endless travelling, suffering and starving that is the lot of the professional cyclist, riding had become a job of work, the joy and promise of those early years lost somewhere along the way. During a Derny race in May 1969 at the Vigorelli Velodrome in Milan, he crashed horrifically at over 80kph. Comatose for two days, Toni suffered life-threatening head injuries, seven broken ribs, four vertebrae, both shoulder blades and a collar bone. *La Gazzetta dello Sport* reported that 'Poor Toni has broken everything that could be broken.' The brilliant career that never quite was ended thus; in calamity and despair amidst the crippled and helpless of a Milanese public hospital.

Toni recovered in time and eventually felt well enough to join Ivana in the family business, a little earlier than planned maybe, but planned all the same. In 2000 the couple retired and their oldest son Davide took over. Four years later Davide's wife walked out on him and Toni and Ivana lost not only their pension but their home, as Davide's depression saw the business collapse.

In 2005 another Turbigese Olympic champion, the Bobsledder Mario Armano, began to canvas the Mayor on behalf of his friend Toni Bailetti, fallen on hard times and living in a tiny one-bedroomed flat with his wife and middle-aged son. Assistance was sought from the CONI, the Italian Olympic committee and in March 2006 Toni received a letter of recognition and his first monthly 'Olympic Pension' cheque. Toni hopes to move to a larger apartment sometime in 2008.

Davide Bailetti is back in work, back on his bike and, when we meet, has the look of a man who has been through the very worst of times but who is discovering how to live his life. He is courteous, charming and evidently happy. His mother and father are immensely proud of him.

STAGE FIVE

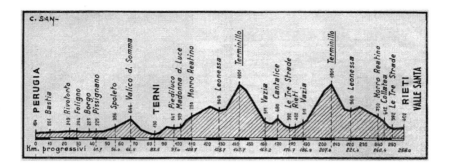

On stage five the Giro continued south into the Lazio region for two ascents of Rome's great mountain, the fearsome Terminillo, at 1,900 metres amongst the biggest of the Appenine range, before concluding at Rieti, the geographical centre of Italy. The Appenines, traditionally under-used in the Giro, stretch from north to south for over 1,600 kilometres to form the backbone of the peninsular. Thirty kilometres out of Perugia, some 228 from the finishing line, a stocky, unknown Frenchman named Joseph Carrara, riding for Henri Anglade's Liberia-Grammont team, suffered a slow puncture. Rather than drop out of the back of the listless peloton, Carrara, eighteenth on GC at 3'48", decided instead to accelerate away, thus creating a lead sufficient to facilitate a quick bike change before being re-absorbed by the group. This way he would avoid being shelled out in the unlikely event of someone being foolhardy enough to attack so early in such a long, demanding stage. Nothing unusual in this, Carrara made his excuses, clipped away off the front, changed bike and promptly rejoined the pack.

Minutes later Carrara, the 24-year-old son of an Italian immigrant father from Bergamo, received word that his original bike, tyre changed, was once more fit for action. Off he went up the road again. Only this time, upon receipt of the repaired bike Joseph Carrara did something quite stupid: he decided not to go back to the peloton but instead, to take off on a hopeless, misguided 220-kilometre game of chicken, much to the bewilderment of his *Directeur Sportif,* Adolphe Deledda – the more so because the two had only met the previous week. The fact was that Carrara wasn't contracted to Liberia at all but was an 'independent', hired at the last minute to make up the numbers in assisting Anglade, an eleventh hour inclusion in the race.

By and by the swarthy looking Carrara, seemingly a useful time trialist, increased his lead until, by the time he crested the Terminillo for the first time at 100 kilometres, he'd extended his advantage to an improbable 11 minutes. The press, disarmed by the fact that they knew absolutely nothing about the new virtual *maglia rosa,* gathered around Jean Bobet, doyenne of the French cycling media and brother of the three times Tour de France winner. Bobet, font of all cycling knowledge, declaimed thus:

'I can exclusively reveal that I'd never set eyes on him before Saturday, though I have been able to establish that he took the 8 o'clock train into Milan.'

And?

'And I understand he may possibly have won some regional races, and that he holds an independent licence. I think he may have nearly won some other races, but I could be wrong. Liberia called him to race because they were struggling for a team and he lives close to the Italian border. I don't know any more. There are probably a hundred and fifty riders like him in France.'

Oh, OK. That's great. Thanks Jean. Thanks a lot.

Carrara held on heroically to win his stage in just under nine hours, though the *maglia rosa* ultimately proved beyond him, as a torpid peloton, led by Suarez's Ghigi team-mates, finally roused itself 50 kilometres from the finish and began the chase. On the second climb Van Looy found himself shelled out of the main bunch, his suspect Grand Tour credentials once more revealed as he lost in excess of ten minutes.

By the time Joseph Carrara collapsed over the line, far too exhausted to shed any more light on precisely who he was and quite what it was he thought he was doing, he had accomplished one of the great exploits of postwar Giro history. The following morning, utterly shattered and unable to stay with the peloton, Carrara climbed off his bike and slipped quietly out of Italy. Bobet had got at least one thing right – his geography. Carrara lives peacefully in Cormaranche en Bugey, a stones throw from the family of Roger Pingeon, winner of the 1967 Tour de France, some 150 kilometres from the Mont Blanc tunnel. Chapeau to him. *Bon courage!*

Joseph Carrara winning Stage 5

STAGE SIX

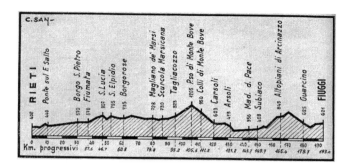

Ten kilometres into the sixth stage, three of the Giro's more useful *rouleurs*, Schroeders of Faema, Pellegrino of Molteni and Sartore of Carpano escaped an uninterested pack and set about building a stage-winning advantage. In truth nobody had much stomach for the chase. Today the break suited the majority within the peloton perfectly, two bruising ascents in foul weather of the Terminillo the previous day having left their mark. Mindful of this, the threesome, working cohesively together, built for themselves an unassailable 12-minute buffer as they crested the big climb of the day, the Monte Bove, at 105 kilometres.

As the race hove within spitting distance of his home town, Vincenzo Meco, three months into his fledgling professional cycling career and keen to strut his not inconsiderable stuff, tried his luck. Meco, the surprise package of the opening week of the Giro (much to Taccone's chagrin), hitched a ride on an opportunist train driven by two wily Giro campaigners, Baffi and Brugnami. Apparently good news for these two as attention-seeking Meco, young, strong and seemingly misguided, set about towing them along at a thunderous pace. On and on he ploughed until Baffi, at the ripe old age of 31 no longer supple enough to push the big gears, disappeared suddenly out of the back door. Not that Meco let this bother him. By the time he led the exhausted Brugnami over the finishing line he'd reduced stage-winner Schroeders' advantage to under two minutes, and in so doing put the thick end of three minutes into the erstwhile race-leader, Suarez.

Thus Vincenzo Meco, a cycling nobody from the cycling backwater of Abruzzo, blasted his way to cycling immortality – *maglia rosa* in the Giro d'Italia.

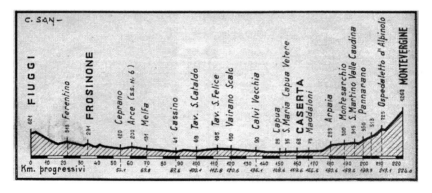

Stage 7

Stage seven, 215 fast, flat, due south kilometres followed by a 12-kilometre ramp up to the old town of Montevergine, found the Giro in the ancient Kingdom of Naples, the very heart of the Mezzogiorno, Italy's deep south. After 170 kilometres a group of ten heavyweights, headed by Van Looy and the Milan–San Remo winner, Daems, bolted clear of the peloton and made for home – a high risk strategy given that the dangerous Carlesi, twelfth at 3'30" and amongst the genuine GC favourites, was amongst their number. Fifteen blood and thunder kilometres later they were caught by what *Tuttosport* described as a 'fire breathing peloton'.

Next to try his hand was the powerful Belgian, Armand Desmet. Liberated from his duties as *gregario* in chief to Van Looy, following the latter's collapse on stage five, Desmet, seventh overall but not considered a contender, was a good wheel to follow. This fact was not lost on Henri Anglade and 25-year-old Giuseppe Sartore of Carpano; both of them immediately latched on. The three escapees barrelled on at 45kmh, hitting the foot of the climb four minutes in advance of the peloton, acutely aware that the last man standing would likely assume stewardship of the pink jersey as well. Elsewhere the big guns again kept their powder dry for fear of going too deep too soon.

Sartore, the fourth of six cycling mad brothers from the Nizza valley, south of Milan, had begun his working life as a farmer before signing for Bianchi in 1960. Though without a win for two injury-plagued seasons, when fit and able he had shown enough promise to earn a place at Carpano with Balmamion. Here though, in the high class company of Anglade and Desmet, he soon found himself out of his depth, cracking on the lower slopes as the two 'Trans-Alpines' cranked up the pace. Half way up, with the gradient steepening, Anglade buckled under Desmet's onslaught, enabling the blond Flemish from the flatlands of Weregem, to punch his way to the top and a double celebration – brilliant stage-winner and worthy *maglia rosa*.

Further down the mountain hostilities finally commenced as Defilippis seized the initiative with 4 kilometres remaining, a quick salvo across the bows of his adversaries. Nino would take ten seconds from Gaul, 22 from Battistini and Taccone, and over half a minute from a group containing Massignan, Nencini and Balmamion. That the time gaps were negligible was, for Nino, largely irrelevant. He knew the Giro couldn't be won in four short kilometres here, far away from the great mountains of the North. Of greater significance, psychologically and physically, was the test itself, however brief.

The motivation for Nino's aggression, regardless of the race position, was manifest. He believed that Massignan, a failure here, was susceptible to the mental strain imposed by his position amongst the favourites, ultimately incapable of winning a Grand Tour. He felt that Taccone, though sporadically brilliant, was headstrong and injudicious, lacking the intelligence and experience to adequately manage his resources, however considerable they might be. Battistini would be too passive in the mountains, far too indecisive to wrest the initiative, too nice a human being to prevail. Pambianco and Nencini lacked the punch of the pure climbers and would suffer badly in the final week. All of which left Charly Gaul, twice previously a winner, but disappointing in finishing only fourth the previous year, and then crushed by Anquetil at the Tour. For all his devastating talent the Luxembourger hated riding in the heat and had always been prone to spectacular collapse. Furthermore he, like Nino himself, was approaching the end of his career, and possibly lacked the hunger, and the legs, to suffer once more at the sharp end of a Grand Tour.

Nino's message then was abundantly clear. The last great buccaneer of Italian cycling was riding not for stage-wins, hearts and flowers. He was riding to win the Giro d'Italia…

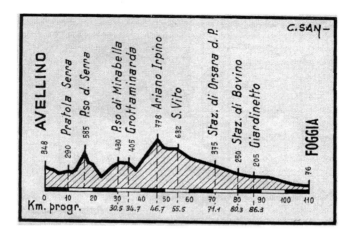

The second Saturday of the Giro comprised a blessedly short (110 kilometre) north-easterly hop from Avellino to the bombed-out, scraped-out, grimly rebuilt Pugliese tenement city of Foggia, optimistically known as the 'Granary of Italy'. Here, on a torpid, clay-hot day the miserable furnace that is Puglia's summer exposed itself in its indolence and poverty of spirit. This is Italy's deep South, feckless, dissolute and amoral, churlishly nurturing its chronic persecution complex. On this most mindless of days the race hurried its way through weary olive groves and fetid, ignorant whitestone Moorish hill towns. Surrounding and embarrassing these lay the area's great shame, the white, windowless conical hovels known as *trulli*. Built by the Moors and latterly inhabited by peasant farmers, the *trulli* now stood crumbling in their thousands throughout their blank, desultory moonscape. Small wonder that these arid, meagre fields found themselves abandoned in favour of the dreary, high-rise living found in the sanitised concrete jungles of Foggia, Taranto and Brindisi. Reinvented and reclaimed in the name of 'heritage' for the twenty-first century by noxious estate agents, the *trulli* have become holiday homes for the cloying new middle classes of Britain and Germany.

Forty kilometres from the finish, Van Looy had his Faema team-mates arrange themselves at the head of the race, allowing Huub Zilverberg to break away in the company of one of Italian cycling's forgotten men, the Florentine, Sante Ranucci. As a talented, brassy 21-year-old, Ranucci had been good enough to win the World Amateur Championship in 1955. Turning professional and unable fully to cope with the burden of expectation, he became overly reliant on stimulants, irreparably damaging his engine – like many of his generation. By 1962 he was a bit-part player at Torpado, one of Italy's bit-part teams. Drafted into the Giro only at the last minute when the veteran *gregario* Pettinati cried off ill, Ranucci never stood a chance here, as Zilverberg, his career path the direct inverse of Ranucci's, easily won their sprint; another good day for Faema and, as the Giro entered its middle week, the first of several easy, inconsequential ones for the GC suitors.

Enrico Peracino in the Carpano team-car, Giro d'Italia, 1962

THE MAN WHO DISCOVERED HOT WATER

In truth it hadn't started at all well with Dr Peracino. With expert timing I'd approached him, a great, inelegant old bear of a man in gaudy psychedelic yellow lycra, as he angrily climbed from his bike at the conclusion of the old lads' club-run. Mechanically extricating himself from an expensive carbon bicycle, massively at odds with himself and his Colnago, he testily agreed to my inane request for a photograph, then, still more aggrieved, hurled the recalcitrant machine roughly, disgustedly into the boot of a large Italian Estate car.

As a (pretty hopeless) amateur cyclist myself, I knew precisely, instinctively how he felt. Classic, telltale symptoms you see, the dismissal of the bike, the self-loathing, the barely concealed rage. In synopsis? He'd looked forward to the ride for weeks, trained hard, suffered interminable hours on an indoor turbo trainer. He'd felt himself to be in good nick, then failed miserably for no apparent reason, ridden through treacle on a bike which not only didn't fit, but which felt completely alien. How he'd loved, cared for and cherished that bike. Everything out of kilter, one leg too long, the other not long enough, the muscles in his groin and hamstrings stretched and painful. The soles of his feet sore from the ill-fitting shoes that had fitted his newly deformed feet perfectly only the night before. A dull ache in his backside. His lungs had deserted him. He'd been pedalling squares. His lower back hurt, everything hurt, his knees hurt, his wrists, the back of his neck and his shoulders.

Sometimes you can't ride, sometimes you're not even good enough to pedal squares. Sometimes it's a mess you're pedalling, confused, dissonant, disconnected, out of control. Yourself, the bike, everything out of kilter. Soul destroying. You're just lurching, thrashing around on the thing, sinking and miserable, the very opposite of kinesis, the very opposite of cycling. Tyres too flat, cranks too long, handlebars too narrow, the wrong gears. Always the wrong gears. Always in the wrong gear. Sometimes the harder you try the worse it gets. Blame everything, everyone. Blame the bike, blame the traffic, blame your colleagues. Ultimately you'll blame yourself. It's your neurosis. You signed up for it when you bought your first racing bike.

It's cycling. You'll be fine. Sometimes it's alright, occasionally it's good, you're good, you *feel* good. *Very* occasionally it's just a wonderful, wondrous thing, the best thing. Then the suffering is euphoric, indescribably good, the best of all things, the absolute nectar. Those are the days. Days like those and the feeling lasts for days. You can walk on water. Those are the days and they're precious, fantastic and expensive, very expensive. Days like those take a lot, a hell of a lot of earning. Days like today are just a small down payment.

He seemed bolshie and full of self-loathing and I didn't dare speak to him. I liked him immediately. He would be fine. I'd try again at lunch.

I try again at lunch and we make another false start, the mother of all false starts. He sits on the balcony with the rest of the smokers, studiously filling his pipe as the others, the flyweights and bantams, playfully and excitedly spar at being young again. Five old friends arm wrestling in Piedmontese, their curiously tongue twisted hybrid, Franco-Italian. He's with them and of them but he isn't *one of them*. They're ex-cyclists, cut by and large from the same coarse cloth. He is something other, something measured, substantive and contained. One spare seat at the table, one just landed Englishman. Sod it. I've had three hours of verbal assault and battery, sensory overload from an old guy who used to make cycling shoes for Eddy Merckx. I've *earned* my smoke. Now, suddenly, I'm rolling a cigarette in this desperate, interminable silence. I'm in Italy to speak with cyclists and I've rendered them silent, rendered them awkward and uncomfortable at their own reunion.

Just when you think it can't get any worse Peracino, in English and by way of an ice-breaker asks 'What do you want?' in just precisely the way you'd ask the bailiff. And I feel besieged. I feel like I'm being accused of something and I explain as best I can that I really need a smoke and that the shoemaker Battilossi talks and talks, and I'm here to interview Balmamion, and I'm sorry because my Italian is a disaster, and are you all Torinese, and oh, you're Guido Messina from Sicily it's an honour to meet you – and I'm turning to Peracino and asking if he'd worked for Carpano, and I'm thinking that's killed some time at least not long to go and Peracino says in his baritone that he was the Doctor of Carpano, and he and I are talking and it's almost a conversation of sorts. And the poor bugger is saddled with the dim Englishman and the others are back about their business, and I'm thinking that 'What do you want?' wasn't accusatory at all, but probably the only English he could muster and that Italians say 'Cosa vuoi?' all the time and literally translated it means as near as makes no difference 'What would you like?' and it's not at all impolite, it's what the baker or the person in the shoe shop asks you and actually it's the opposite of impolite. And I'm thankful because he's obviously a kind man with an innate intelligence, and absolutely typical Piedmontese and he'll have a story to tell, but he won't volunteer it because he's reticent and Piedmontese and...

*　*　*　*

In December 1959 the great French rider, Raphael Geminiani, invited the *Campionissimo* Coppi, Jacques Anquetil and another three of the more notable French riders to ride a lucrative exhibition race in Upper Volta (now Burkina Faso), the West African colony celebrating its newly won independence from France. Following the race, Coppi and Geminiani spent a listless, uncomfortable, mosquito ravaged evening at the palatial villa of a local construction magnate. The following day, out on a hunting expedition, Fausto Coppi developed a raging fever.

Arriving home in Piedmont on December 18 he was jaundiced and exhausted. By Boxing Day he was bedridden, vomiting and complaining of a chronic, unquenchable thirst. Wife Giulia, suspecting malaria, called the family doctor, Ettore Allegri, who testily agreed to see the stricken champion. Allegri made a cursory visit that afternoon and immediately diagnosed flu. Prescribing rest, mineral water and a mild course of camphor, Allegri dismissed as hysterical nonsense Giulia's suggestion that her husband may have contracted malaria in Africa. There would be no blood test. Three days later, as Coppi's condition continued to deteriorate, Giulia sought a second opinion from Professor Giovanni Astaldi, a close friend who had treated her husband successfully for Typhus two years earlier. Astaldi confirmed Allegri's diagnosis – the Campionissimo had viral flu.

On New Years day Allegri was again summonsed to the emaciated champion. With Coppi desperately ill he changed his diagnosis to 'unknown' and had him transferred to hospital in Tortona. Meanwhile, across the border in Clermont Ferrand Geminiani, poleaxed by precisely the same symptoms, insisted on a blood test, convinced he had contracted malaria. When the Pasteur institute confirmed Gem's self-diagnosis he immediately had his brother telephone Astaldi with the news. Astaldi, adamant now that Coppi was suffering from pneumonia, told him in no uncertain terms to mind his own business. Inexplicably and tragically

Coppi was prescribed the immunosuppressant cortisone, hastening his demise. He died the following morning. Raphael Geminiani survived.

The loss of her greatest sportsman, the sheer futility, not only traumatised Italy but shook the sport of cycling to its very foundations. Notwithstanding the fact that Coppi's death was not directly attributable to racing, the damaging, debilitating nature of the sport was brought sharply into focus. Cycling, the hardest of all endurance sports, with its inhuman workloads and ingrained doping culture, contemplated its collective naval.

*　*　*　*

In 1953 Sir Edmund Hillary's first successful ascent of Everest fired the global imagination, and that of a gifted 20-year-old medical student named Enrico Peracino. That winter one of his lecturers, similarly inspired by Hillary's achievement, formed a study group to measure the heart's response under intense physical strain. Peracino, an accomplished amateur cyclist, immediately agreed to participate. Here he met fellow guinea pigs, Nino Defilippis and Angelo Conterno, the brightest young stars in the Torinese cycling firmament, and the three became good friends.

Peracino, oldest of eight children, was born into medicine. Both his father and paternal uncle were doctors, as was his late wife, Anna. As a young man he'd contemplated a career in cycling (he was a more than useful sprinter), the great passion of his life. However, all too familiar with the tenuous nature of the sport and of its harmful consequences, Enrico, to his father's immense relief, wisely chose University and financial security over the glory and potential physical ruination offered by a brief career on two wheels. He graduated in 1958, aged 25. Two years later, Coppi's death saw Carpano's two great luminaries demanding that the management enlist the services of Turin's youngest doctor to assist in their preparation and recovery. Vincenzo Giacotto, ambitious, forward thinking and unencumbered by cycling tradition, didn't require a great deal of persuasion. At the age of only 27 Enrico Peracino became the world's first dedicated 'Sports Doctor'.

I ring him in January and arrange to meet in April. He seems surprised and delighted, delicately conjuring his English as I chisel away in Italian; ten magical minutes on Europe's greasy pole of languages, hands across the ocean.

A week or so later, thumbing through an issue of the French weekly *Le Miroir des Sports*, dated August 1960, I find an article describing a meeting between Peracino and Pierre Dumas, then the official (and only permitted) doctor of the Tour de France. The Tour had been won for the third time in succession by a foreigner, Carpano's Gastone Nencini. The piece, by one Andre Chassaignon, is entitled 'Danger of death for the champions used as guinea pigs!' It refers obliquely to 'certain preparations' taken by the Belgium and Italian riders, and reports 'a passionate though cordial debate about the moral and ethical responsibilities of the doctors'.

Following his success at the 1957 Giro, Nencini had been decidedly ordinary the following year, then endured a wretched season in 1959, finishing a distant tenth at the *corsa rosa*, almost 14 minutes in arrears of Charly Gaul. In 1960, under the guidance of Peracino at Carpano, 30-year-old Nencini's form underwent a dramatic improvement as he came within 30 seconds of unseating Anquetil at the Giro. Riding for the national team at the Tour, he become only the fourth Italian to carry the *maillot jaune* into Paris, after the earlier race-leader, Rivière, fell into a ravine and broke his back. What's more, Carpano's contingent of Belgiam and Italian riders won an unprecedented seven stages, whilst another Italian in Dr Peracino's care, Graziano Battistini, claimed a further two.

I finally get to meet Enrico Peracino in the honeysuckled garden of his handsome villa set in the hills overlooking Turin, in the company of his beautiful, thoughtful daughter Paola, Franco Balmamion and Vin Denson, the remarkable English *domestique* who won a stage at the 1966 Giro. Like Balmamion and Peracino, Vin had been on the Ventoux when his best friend, Tom Simpson, died in 1967. Mindful of the fact that doping remains the great *omerta* of professional cycling, I'm wary of discussing the article, particularly in view of Paola's presence. I want to know, however, the role Peracino had played in the successes of Nencini and Balmamion, in the Carpano story and in doping, cycling's endless self-delusion. Peracino, though caught off guard by the article, seems more than happy to relive the events of the time, to share his memories.

'I remember that meeting with Dr Dumas well; it took place in a hotel after the Izoard stage. Binda, the Italian Team Manager, had asked me to help out at the Tour, and of course it was a dream for me. The journalist suggests there was conflict between me and Dumas, but this was not the case at all; we were on good terms and became firm friends. Dumas and his two assistants were stretched to breaking point that year. He was happy for me to look after the Italian team and the Belgium riders of Carpano. Giacotto and I followed the Tour in my car, ostensibly as tourists. The organizers didn't permit us to travel with the team in an official capacity, so it was really a crazy time, sneaking into the team Hotel after dark.'

Why then the suggestion that the Italians were in some way 'prepared'? Why the sneaking around after dark, the clandestine meetings?

'The French put two and two together and came up with five. Remember that this was the third time in succession they'd failed to win their national Tour and the public demanded to know why. It suited their purposes to imply that we were up to no good, but it was pretty hypocritical. They wanted to know what we were doing, why our riders were so strong. The fact was that we had simply discovered "hot water".'

Now I'm confused.

'In Italy if you say you discovered hot water it means you didn't discover anything at all. It's a play on words. The riders were drinking up to ten litres of water a day on the hotter stages, often from contaminated mountain springs. They were re-hydrating without replacing any of the minerals lost as they sweated. I simply put them on saline drips, restoring the mineral balance, and ensured they ate the right foods in sufficient quantities. I helped them to understand their bodies. It was only 200cc, but they recovered better and slept better.'

Given his candour I ask him outright whether he considered it doping.

'I never doped them. If they chose to dope themselves that was their business, and many, particularly the Belgians, did. I was a doctor; my concern was their health. The object of the exercise was to help them to *not dope*, though many of the riders felt that it was just a part of their job, entirely unsanctioned until Simpson died in '67. Sadly most didn't understand the correlation between health and performance. On occasions I would check their pockets before a stage and find syringes and pills, usually amphetamine and other 'brain exciters' like pervatin. It wasn't quite as rampant then as people would have you believe, but as the decade wore on, as Italian riders joined Belgian teams, and vice versa, the climate changed and doping really proliferated.'

He explains that Nencini ate prodigiously in an era when large meals were still thought to impair and not aid performance, and when amphetamine was considered useful as an appetite suppressant. Why, I ask, has Nencini become infamous for and synonymous with doping?

'Let me give you an example of what we were fighting against at the 1960 Tour. Nencini had a huge appetite; he loved to eat. During that Tour, on the eve of a mountain stage he ate a massive meal – three steaks – despite my protests. I told him I thought he was crazy and that if he felt ill in the morning he should go to the Aspro [ambulance] and not to bother me. The following morning he went to the ambulance with indigestion. That evening he told me he'd seen many of the French riders injecting themselves at the Aspro. Then the following day it was all around the peloton that Nencini had been seen doping! The notion that Nencini was a big doper was a French construct. The fact is that many of the riders – French, Italian, Belgian – were. These stories tend to gather legs.'

Nencini died in 1980, aged only 50. 'An easy target'.
Did the Doctor feel his presence had offered the Carpano riders an unfair advantage?

'Perhaps, though in truth I didn't distinguish between Carpano riders and the others for the most part. Carpano paid my wages, but I tried to be available to all of the riders, from all of the teams. I loved the work, and Giacotto had no problem with that. It was in everyone's interest for the riders to be healthy. My job was to help them to be more healthy.'

Peracino. Giacotto and the journalist, Ruggero Radice

After Carpano's withdrawal from cycling in 1964, Peracino followed his great friend Giacotto, first to Sanson, then in 1967 to Faema. Giacotto had secured the services not only of Vittorio Adorni but also the precocious Belgian, Eddy Merckx, and insisted that Peracino be entrusted with their wellbeing. They would work successfully together for three years. At the 1969 Giro Merckx, the runaway leader, famously tested positive for the stimulant 'Reactivan' at Savona, and was ejected from the race, the first high profile victim of the more stringent anti-doping controls introduced in the wake of Simpson's death. Predictably enough he has always proclaimed his innocence (as did Dr Peracino), claiming that he was spiked. Notwithstanding the fact that Merckx would fail a further dope test in Italy at the 1973 Tour of Lombardy, the overwhelming suspicion remains that, spiked or not, Merckx – the only positive in a race lousy with amphetamine – was victimised for turning the Giro into a monotonous procession for the second time in succession.

The previous year several big-name riders, amongst them Balmamion, Motta and Gimondi, had tested positive. Tellingly, none of the Italian favourites were disqualified. More tellingly still, the 1969 Giro was won by an Italian, Felice Gimondi. The 'Savona affair', as it's become known, is perhaps cycling's greatest unsolved mystery, and continues to fascinate the cycling conspiracy theorists of both Italy and Belgium. Like all great unsolved cases everybody claims to know who did it but, in the best cycling tradition, nobody's telling, and that's exactly as it should be. Round and round and round it goes, *ad infinitum*.

At dinner, I cleverly, casually enquire of Enrico Peracino whether he recalls what happened.

'Yes of course. I know exactly what happened. I was there.'

'What happened?'

'Yes. I know exactly what happened.'

'Does Merckx know what happened?'

'Eddy knows exactly what happened.'

'And what did? What did happen?'

'Oh, you want to what *happened*?'

(He's enjoying his English now, thinks he's playing me. He is.)

'Yes Enrico. I want to know what *actually* happened.'

'What *actually* happened was that Eddy was obliged to leave the race.'

'Pass me the carrots please, Doctor'.

By 1967 Peracino's stock was so great that when Nino Benvenuti challenged Emile Griffith for the World Middleweight Championship, Italy's greatest ever boxer enlisted his services for the fight – a 15-round Madison Square Garden epic, famously won by the visitor. Upon Giacotto's untimely death in 1970 Peracino retired from his position, as Merckx's departure to Molteni coincided with the decline of Piedmontese cycling. Now family and work commitments took precedence over cycling. In 1976, aged 43, he became the youngest ever Primary of Radiology at Turin's Molinette Hospital. Later, he worked extensively for the city's two great soccer teams. In the early-80s he advised Juventus on dietary matters, before a spell with Torino during the club's all too brief renaissance of the early-90s. He continued to advise bike-racers in an unofficial, ad hoc capacity before abandoning cycling altogether when blood doping and EPO began to deform the sport into the appalling, unedifying charade we witness today. What did he think of modern cycling?

'In all honesty I'm sickened by much of it. It's no longer a sport; it's something entirely different. It's science fiction and the public understands this. That's why cycling is in crisis. I feel desperately sorry for today's cyclists, their health and performance hijacked, manipulated and controlled by doctors. Their destiny is to die young, to pay with their lives – a tragedy. I've had the parents of 15 and 16-year-old boys knocking on my office door asking me for medical products for their sons, demanding that I help them to become professional racers – unbelievable! Let's hope that the next generation have a chance to enjoy this sport without doping. It's true that the riders always doped – they would take amphetamine because they knew no better – but they never tried to change their physiology, as they do today. They doped because they didn't know any different; teams were small and the races harder, longer and more frequent. Look at Balmamion and Defilippis, look at the Carpano riders from the 50s and 60s. For the most part they are well, and healthy. Angelo Conterno suffered a brain haemorrhage last January. By May he was back on his bike and by the end of November he'd ridden 3,000 kilometres, aged 81.'

For almost half a century since the great Giri of the early 60s, Italian cycling has produced a procession of riders, often of dubious moral and sporting virtue, who have been lionised for achievements considerably less noteworthy than those of Balmamion and his generation.

Even today, in an age in which it's impossible to take cycling's grand tour contenders seriously as credible athletes, in any naïve, Corinthian, ultimately meaningful sense, cycling fans are prepared to kid themselves that what, and who, they are witnessing is in some way relevant, that the protagonists are 'real' sportsmen. The reality of course is that these extraordinarily gifted, extraordinarily dedicated young men have been betrayed by the beautiful but filthy whore of a sport that cycling has become. Since blood doping and later EPO was found to transform athletic performance in the early 90s, stage-race cycling has mutated into a Pandora's box full to bursting with synthetic hormone, transfused blood, Insulin Growth factor and testosterone. To see the astonishing speeds at which today's cyclists ride up mountains is to witness at first hand a hopeless, broken distortion, a parody of competition. Viewed with contempt by the wider sporting community, abhorred by the anti-doping agencies, cycle-racing is now viewed as the hopelessly drug-addicted pariah of world sport, poisoned by intransigent team-managers and myopic race organizers. Shamefully the sport has become a laughing stock for those rational enough to have long ago ceased to care. Meanwhile, a deluded, well-meaning minority frets and worries that bike racing will recover its former glories; rose-tinted carers assisting the euthanasia of western Europe's great sporting heritage, a betrayal and a travesty.

Enrico Peracino revolutionised cycling. You've never heard of him? Neither had I. Neither, by and large, has anyone else outside of the tiny universe within a universe which was the Italian peloton in the 1960s and early-70s. But revolutionise the sport he did, albeit quite unwittingly, for better or worse. After four challenging, enjoyable hours in his company the question of doping seems more opaque than ever, still a bundle of contradictions and ambiguities.

The Doctor's lack of contrition should come as no surprise: Carpano acted within the laws of a brutal, unforgiving sport, such as they were before doping became the runaway train on which Tom Simpson rode to his death in July 1967. What's more, his relationship with his riders and his status within the medical community leave little doubt that his morality and professional integrity were unimpeachable. This was no charlatan masquerading as a health professional, but a dedicated physician who happened to love cycling, and cyclists. He cared for them, and about them. The more pertinent question – perhaps the only question – is whether he acted within the spirit of cycling, and of sport. My belief, for what it's worth, is that the answer lies in a small memorial a kilometre or so from the top of Mont Ventoux, and in the continued good health of riders like Nino Defilippis and Franco Balmamion, Piedmontese by accident of birth and, 45-odd years on, still close friends of Enrico Peracino.

Enrico Peracino died thirteen days after our interview. This book is dedicated to his memory and to his legacy.

STAGE NINE

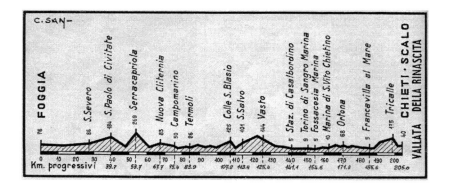

Following its loop around the surly, unemployed villages of the 'Mezzogiorno', the grateful peloton turned sharply and readily north towards the Adriatic coast, aiming once more for the traditional heartlands of the Giro. In so doing our heroes skirted a mountainous, brooding terrain, all dry stone and primitive menace. Inarticulate and wild, the Abruzzo is the northernmost outcrop of Southern Italy, a craggy hinterland worshipped and abandoned in equal measure by ancient, one-eyed Luddite tribes. Untamed and implacable, the area is synonymous with hardship, its communities notoriously insular and suspicious.

In the western Abruzzo lies the town of Avezzano, birthplace not only of Vincenzo Meco but also of Vito Taccone, the 'Chamois of Abruzzo'. Of all of the misfortunes to have befallen Abruzzo's citizens down the centuries, the 1915 earthquake, which claimed the lives of over 12,000 *Avezzani,* remains the most appalling. Though rebuilt after a fashion, Avezzano remained for decades a metaphor for Abruzzo's seemingly hopeless malaise. According to the National Office of Statistics, the average GDP in 1962 was little over 50 per-cent of that of Rome, 100 kilometres or so to the west, but a universe away culturally and economically. EU money, huge government grants for inward investment, better roads and latterly tourism have dramatically improved the lot of Abruzzo in recent years, but the area remains quintessentially Southern Italian in character; obstinate, solitary and unyielding.

Here, in the dark, unspeakable underbelly of the 'Bel Paese', Taccone's greedy, insistent character was formed during a fatherless upbringing characterised by the most punishing of all childhood privations – real, genuine hunger. In winning a stage at his first Giro in 1961 Vito earned enough to pay off, at a single stroke, a lifetime of accumulated family debt. The 500,000 lire he took home was equivalent to nearly three years' income in the Taccone family. Small wonder then that he had little time for the mannered chit-chat of the peloton; Vito Taccone was in it for the money.

Confronted by the cold chill of Abruzzo's abandonment, the Giro dared not leave the sanctuary of the shoreline, enabling Faema to hold the peloton in check once more. Rik Van Looy easily prevailed in the mass sprint for the finish as his team tightened its stronghold on the race with a fourth consecutive stage-win.

Vito Taccone and Vincenzo Meco

Walter Martin in the Motovelodromo di Torino after winning the Milan–Torino

... and being congratulated by Mum and Dad

THE UNSTOPPABLE WALTER MARTIN

Saturday 11th March 1961. 3p.m.
Motovelodromo di Torino, Corso Casale, Turin.

On the breakneck descent of the Superga, towards the conclusion of the Milano–Torino bicycle-race, two local riders have escaped the peloton. They are 24-year-old Walter Martin of Carpano and, wearing the granata of Turin's 'second' cycling team Baratti, the veteran Angelo Conterno. A sardined, sweaty velodrome places its bets for Turin's cycling derby.

Martin, a Toro fan in a black and white jersey, is a young man on the verge of a breakthrough, unfettered, bold and fearless. Crowd favourite Conterno, still remarkably competitive two days short of his 36th birthday, retains the boyish, disarming good looks of the courtesan. With his elegant blond coiffure and impeccable road manners he is *Penna Bianca*, the 'white feather' of Torinese cycling. In the back straight, Conterno, readying himself for the headrush of the sprint, floats astutely to the top of the steep banking, the watchtower of the velodrome. And, in that fraction, as his right leg cramps, is sunk. Martin, incendiary in his readiness, drives his power down through the frame and sprints emphatically and comprehensively to his first major victory and a renewed, improved contract. Reward for winning the fastest ever single-day bike-race and for the fast twitch, revisionist elasticity of youth.

Saturday 13th July 1964. 8.15p.m.
Motovelodromo di Torino, Corso Casale, Turin.

A balmy summer's evening, a prestigious, packed-to-the-rafters exhibition track meeting on the eve of the final stage of the Tour de France, a night at the opera for the proletariat. A four-kilometre two-man pursuit featuring, in the home straight modest, mannered 27-year-old Walter Martin, former winner of Milan–Torino, here paired with Olympic team pursuit gold medallist and World Record holder,

Valentino Gasparella. Opposing them, in the back straight, we have the inimitable, inspirational Nino Defilippis, still the biggest draw in Piedmontese cycling, partnered by another Olympic Champion trackman, one Giuseppe Beghetto. Beer money (50,000 lire – £17) and an easy public relations exercise for the Carpano pair, big, necessary money for the two gladiators.

At the gun Gasparella, a body builder on a racing cycle, grenades his bike forward. Martin, a roadman unused to the vortex, unaccustomed to the ferocity and the din and the *maelstrom*, adheres his front wheel, adheres his eyes and his trust and his being to a six-inch airspace behind the champion's back tyre. By the time they round the first bend the gear is turning itself and they're tobogganing, cleaving the air silver. As they hit the back straight the air is all but retired hurt, given up the pretence of resistance, scurrying for cover in neurotic, petulant retreat. Bullied into vapour. Gasparella and Martin are flying, hitting over 60kph, quicksilver. Six inches. Never more than six inches. Never more than six inches. Never more th...

A timekeeper. The kind of individual who keeps time at bike races. Wanting what? A better view? Reckons he can make it from the bottom to the top of the track, reckons he has time enough to get out of Gasparella's way. He hasn't. Gasparella is a World Record holder giving it everything, gunning it for the money. The champion though has ridden hundreds of these exhibitions, has a sixth sense for the pedants in blazers, the catastrophists of cycling officialdom. He sees this one coming, swerves instinctively and suddenly, gets out of *his* way. He probably shouts something, but Martin's hearing, in principle at least surplus to requirements, is out of service tonight and he sees nothing but a wheel, nothing but a wheel and the six inches. Then, momentarily, Martin sees everything. He sees a grey trousered leg with a black shoe attached, some spectators' mouths opened in horror. He sees that he is parallel to and six inches from the track. Then he sees the leather helmet he had been wearing, his left hand, his back wheel somersaulting him, one of his escaping teeth. He sees a kaleidoscope and finally, for the briefest of brief milliseconds, he sees nothing. Then he ceases to see nothing, ceases to hear and feel nothing, for sixteen days. Walter Martin has banged his head, quadruple fractured his skull. Walter Martin is in a coma. Walter Martin has become nothing.

'The crash happened just here, just past half way up the back straight. My life stopped. My life… stopped.'

We're at the velodrome. Mario, myself and Walter Martin. Mario is the kindly, chain-smoking 50-year-old son of Enrico Peracino. He's generously agreed to take a weekend off waiting for the beginning of the cycling season, and to drive around Northern Italy meeting and decoding old cyclists. He's a godsend, a *gregario di lusso*, and a mine of useful information. Only don't get him on Eddy Merckx. He'll talk for hours about Merckx. Mario was a cycling-obsessed 13-year-old in 1964 and remembers the crash well, remembers the phone call and his father's anguish. He remembers the torment, the desolation and the prayers, the bedside vigils for Walter. Mario's sister had told me that Walter momentarily loses his spatial awareness, often repeats himself. For a number of reasons this may be a difficult two hours for Mario.

Walter Martin has his right leg in a pot and is cheerfully struggling to walk. He's fallen off his bike again. The last time I saw him his wrist was in pot following a fall. Walter's always falling off. While I speculate on why he has no index finger on his left hand, Walter starts telling me the story of the day he fell off and lost two litres of blood, about the time he couldn't recognise his mother for over a month, about the neurosurgery and the short-term memory loss. He's telling me about the mental blackouts he still suffers today, the lost sense of smell and time and place, and the resultant falling-off. He's telling me without a hint of bitterness or resentment. He's thrilled that I'd be interested. How could I not be interested? The people you like are always interesting. More than anything I want to tell his story, to preserve something of his life in cycling. If that sounds pompous and conceited then so be it. People like Walter Martin, humble and damaged and old, are the story of the great years of European cycling.

As we enter the velodrome Walter thanks the gateman, a handsome and uninterested youth of about 20. He tells him that he used to race here from time to time. He neglects to tell him that he won the world's fastest ever bike race here and that the place almost cost him his life. Mario tells the gateman he's Walter Martin, winner of Milan–Turin.

The boy very politely feigns interest, but evidently hasn't the faintest idea what we're talking about.

Walter was born in 1936, of Piedmontese parentage in Ostia Lido, near Rome on the Tyrrhenian coast. In 1943, fearful of the American assault at nearby Anzio, his family evacuated north to Turin. Here he fell in love with the sport of cycling, though it took him fully three races to fall off and break his first collarbone. He tells us how he watched in awe as a bike-race flew by the hospital window. Thereafter, when Walter raced and managed to stay upright, he tended to win.

He was very, very fast. By aged 19 he was already amongst the best elite riders in Turin, a city of perhaps 20 cycling clubs. The following year he was competing (and occasionally winning) nationally, locking horns with Ercole Baldini, Arnaldo Pambianco and Bruno Milesi, the class of '36 waiting for the great leap forward. He signed his first professional contract for San Pellegrino, managed by Gino Bartali, in 1958. What had he thought of Bartali?

'I idolised him, much more than Coppi. He was a great rider and a good man, but as a manager he was hopeless, a lousy communicator. All he ever taught us was 'push, push, push'. I suppose that's all he knew, all he needed to know. San Pellegrino was a famous name, but a strange team. They generally only took first-year riders, and in those days you only ever signed for them for a single year. If you succeeded you moved on to another team, if you didn't you were back amongst the elites. We were paid the minimum wage (50,000 lire per month) and were barely a team at all, but the publicity value of Bartali was great, so they got maximum exposure for minimal outlay. They were pretty astute. Anyway I did OK. I nearly won a stage at the Giro and managed to finish it, though I soon realised I wasn't the climber I'd thought I was. I did enough to get a contract with Carpano.'

What was life like as a *gregario* to Defilippis and Nencini?

'It was hard, but manageable. I loved the job and I was lucky enough to be able to afford to do it.'

'*Afford* to do it?'

'In the first year Giacotto didn't select me for the Giro, which was a big disappointment for me, financially and professionally. I needed the money and the chance to shine. Carpano was already a kind of 'super team'; we had a large budget, like Ignis. Even I earned reasonably good money. Most teams had the bare minimum ten to thirteen riders but we had nearly 30, so effectively we pretty much always had two teams on the road. If you were outstanding you raced, but if you weren't you didn't. If you didn't race you didn't really earn a great deal, as simple as that. Every year there were always five or six riders at Carpano who never raced. How they made a living I'll never know. As a *gregario* you knew that if you didn't perform you didn't race.

Our life was expensive. We were obliged to eat a lot of beef, and beef was expensive. We drove all over Europe, which was expensive. The reason many of the riders had short careers, particularly in the smaller teams, was because they couldn't afford to be cyclists. We were all chasing a dream, but many of them would have been better off in a factory. There were riders, good riders, in poorer teams, who retired early because they just ran out of money.'

What role did Giacotto have in mind for him?

'I had no particular role – just to be quiet and race. Giacotto's attitude was that if he had all the best riders under contract then they couldn't be winning races for someone else. That's why we had decent riders kicking their heels. He wanted to create the best team he could, built around the captains. Giacotto, Nencini, Conterno and Defilippis would generally decide who raced where. I had no say in where I went. They'd send me to the Tour of Flanders and Paris–Roubaix knowing full well I didn't have a hope in hell of surviving the cobbles, but someone had to go and do it because Carpano was trying to crack the Begium market. I went because I was Walter Martin, a nobody.

There was a big race in March 1960, the Grand Prix de Nice. Coming into the finish there was a small group and I knew I'd win. I'd trained really hard through the winter and I was the best sprinter in the group. My team-mate, Nencini, offered me 100,000 lire, quite a lot of money, to give him the win. I'd never won a big race before so I told him I wasn't selling. I beat Gastone easily in the sprint by over a wheel length, then waited to be called to the podium. I was awarded second place.'

'Why?'

'Cycling was a business and Nencini was good for business, good for publicity. I wouldn't have minded, but I didn't get the money either! I have the photograph at home of me crossing the line first, winning the race!'

Giacotto again overlooked him for the Giro. Did he consider looking for a new team?

'Not really. I could have been a leader, or perhaps a co-leader, in a smaller team. But I would have been earning less. I just put my head down and rode. Giacotto could be pretty hard sometimes. I was a decent cyclo-cross rider; I finished third in the National Championships and fancied a crack at the World Championships, but Giacotto refused to let me go. He knew, as I did, that I couldn't *win* the Worlds, so as he saw it there was nothing in it for Carpano.'

That June Walter earned another significant win – a stage at the Tour of Switzerland. Did Giacotto's attitude begin to change as he became a winner in his own right?

'No. He and I were never friends. After I won Milan–Turin they had to give me a pay rise (to 170,000 lire, nearly £60 per month), but I think it was the least I deserved. I flogged my guts out for Carpano. I always knew my place with Giacotto. I wasn't a star, a big winner like Franco or Nino, and his attitude was that I ought to think myself lucky. If I'd packed it in there would have been a long queue of riders wanting to take my place. In reality I *was* lucky. A lot of blokes earned less than half of what I got.'

'What happened after the crash?'

'There was the usual court case over compensation. Carpano had two insurance policies, one with the Italian Cycling Federation and another with the City of Torino, the owners of the Velodrome. To be honest though I was only interested in getting back on the bike. I was desperate to ride again, but everyone around me seemed less optimistic. I soon realized it was over for me. My injuries wouldn't allow me to go back to competitive racing. I still dreamt of riding, but I knew it was finished with Carpano. I was 27 when I crashed, no longer a spring chicken. I hadn't had a big win since Milan–Turin and Giacotto was running a business. There was no sentiment whatsoever from him.'

Did Carpano look after him financially, help him to rebuild his life?

'Are you kidding? Forget it! Carpano, or Carpano's insurance company, paid me a million lire, six months' wages. That was half of the settlement the team received. And that was that. The publicity value of the crash alone was probably worth that. Giacotto organised a few track meets, but I never saw any of the money, and nor did I expect to. The money never really bothered me in that sense though. What upset me most was that I was pretty well abandoned. I had huge medical bills and no money. I couldn't work. I couldn't ride.'

Paola had told me in her incomparably beautiful, Italian-girl-speaking-BBC-English voice that Walter is 'in many ways a little like a child', that he had never fully recovered his bearings, which was why he was apt to repeat himself on occasions. Walter is repeating himself now. He keeps telling me that after the crash he couldn't ride his bike for three years. When I press him he distractedly answers my questions about the repeated neurosurgery, the crushing financial hardship, the near unsupportable strain on his marriage. Now, when Walter is obliged to talk about these things, he does so in cursory, agitated ripostes, like we need to hurry up and get back to the point. I try to explain that these things *are* the point, or at least a significant part of the point. Walter respectfully waits for me to finish dripping on about all these irrelevancies, but it's obvious that for some strange reason he doesn't get it. Only now Mario, too, is looking at me with increasingly frustration. His eyebrows are raised and his mouth is open, like he doesn't understand why I'm not able to shut my stupid mouth and *listen*. He's trying to tell me that Walter is *telling me something*. What Walter is telling me is that he couldn't ride his bike for three years. What Walter is telling me is that the coma and the surgery and the breakdown and the stop of life were actually side issues, symptomatic of something infinitely more profound and debilitating. What Walter is telling me is that he *couldn't ride his bike*.

Walter Martin eventually found his bike again in 1966, about the same time he went back to work. In 1970 he found a decent job at Fiat Aerospace, where he would continue until he retired in 1994.

Some 50 yards down and across the road from the Velodrome there is a small, tidy looking café. We decide on a coffee and a warm to conclude our interview (though once inside I push the boat out and, enhancing my reputation as the original wild man of cycling, have tea with milk). Corso Casale is busy this Saturday morning with insistent, impatient traffic, an urgent stream of early morning defectors from the city, eager for the sanity and equanimity of family and the weekend. This is when it happens. Walter, his gaze firmly on where it is he's going, fails to notice the pedestrian crossing 20 yards to his left, the speeding tonnes of metal either side of him, the universe beyond the café door. He begins to stride dangerously and purposefully across the four lanes of traffic as Mario, I and the (mercifully alert) middle-aged woman in the black BMW look on in incredulous, cardiac horror.

Coming to as he completes his maniac crossing, Walter stares back quizzically to where Mario and I remain, rooted and agog. Then, by way of apology and, I think, a tiny thanksgiving, Walter shrugs his shoulders, touches his spectacles with his surviving index finger and smiles his generous, childish smile. He knows he's used up another life, though he doesn't let it trouble him unduly; he stopped counting years ago. Because his brain works 100% perfectly only 99% of the time, Walter not only falls off his bike often but is prone to all manner of accidents and near misses, making him a constant worry to friends and family. He doesn't much mind the bangs and crashes, the minor ops and lay-offs, he's used to them by now. He knows there's probably another one around the corner, but they'll not stop him.

He is Walter Martin, the winner of Milano–Torino. He's 70 years old and on a good day he can still ride his bike at over 50kmh. His world is kind and good and benign. This Walter Martin is a cyclist. Nothing can stop him now.

Walter Martin, 2007

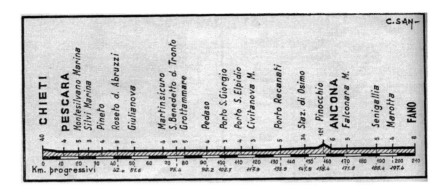

The following day, a perfectly flat, innocuous looking 218 kilometres along the Adriatic coast to lovely, historic Fano, again found Franco Balmamion in the right break, as eight escapees, none apparently significant in the great scheme, sought the prestige and lifelong minor local celebrity a Giro stage-win bestows. Of the eight only Balmamion, already thought peripheral to the main event, was riding for overall classification.

The attack, initiated by Gazzola's Dino Bruni 100 kilometres in, couldn't have suited Faema more perfectly. They had, in Willy Schroeders and in particular the excellent Piet Van Est, the two most accomplished sprinters of the group, a virtual stitch on for the win. Better still though, they found themselves in the company of a naïve, nondescript 24-year-old *gregario* named Giuseppe Tonucci. Tonucci was in his second year as a professional with Italian cycling's richest team, the much hyped but thus far largely anonymous Moschettieri of Pambianco, Nencini and Baldini. Without a win and already showing signs of weakening in the embryonic GC rankings, the Muskateers, more than anyone, needed a stage-win. Lo and behold, and as an outrageous slice of good fortune would have it, young, inspired-for-the-day Tonucci was born in and a native of, of all places, Fano! Incredible or what? Imagine the publicity value Ignis–Moschettieri would garner if Tonucci could only win his first really big race, beating the invincible Flemish in front of his family and friends in his own backyard seaside town! Imagine what a company like Ignis would have to pay for all those 'Local boy makes good' column inches, all that radio coverage, all those photographs in all those big national newspapers. Just imagine what Borghi might pay for that. Just imagine.

Only when the lead grew to an unassailable six minutes did the Faema riders in the main peloton, watchful as ever, begin the long, none too demanding march to save Desmet's *maglia rosa*. Ultimately the breakaway stayed comfortably away, retaining a perfect (for Faema) 90-second advantage. Against all the odds, young Tonucci astounded and delighted the dignitaries sandwiched into Fano's 'Tribune of Honour' (a temporary stand) with a miraculous tyre-width victory. Everyone a winner?

Though Balmamion didn't bother to contest the sprint, he and team-mate Barale did the lion's share of the driving towards the end of the stage. For his troubles Barale earned himself a holiday for two – his reward for winning the intermediate sprint at Ancona. Moreover, Balmamion confirmed his burgeoning authority to Giacotto. He was very strong, and growing stronger by the day. The Canavese, no longer intimidated by Defilippis, now began to nurture aspirations of a top ten finish as the terrible, bullying Dolomites dominated the horizon.

Germano Barale – Carpano's war horse

SATURDAY NIGHT AND SUNDAY MORNING

Saturday night. Torino FC, playing at home in their shiny, soulless new stadium, were extravagantly, reassuringly useless. No shape, no guile, absolutely no guts. The Udinese players, a pretty ordinary bunch themselves, quickly recognized that if they got warm and hung around for ninety minutes a goal would turn up soon enough. Soon enough three turned up, all of them easy and gift-wrapped and cuddly and soft. Balmamion and I agreed that Udinese were good value for the win they'd been gifted, that basically they had done the basics, whatever they are.

Six minutes into the game Barone, one of Toro's massively overpaid midfield dandies, had been presented with what football people commonly refer to as a 'sitter'. Eight yards from goal, unmarked and with the goalkeeper at his mercy, this Barone, apparently a bit-part player in Italy's World Cup winning squad, suffered a kind of brainstorm, blatting the ball with the outside of his left little toe in the general direction of the outer cosmos. This was what's known as a 'howler'. Barone picked himself up, dusted himself down and did something very clever. Having made a howler of his sitter, he proceeded to spend the rest of the game studiously and conscientiously avoiding the ball. It's one of the oldest, hardest tricks in the football book and one at which Barone, with his World Cup winner's pedigree, was particularly adept. The general idea, as I understand it, is that the player should trot around the pitch ostensibly chasing the ball but never quite catching up with it, ergo never having to kick it, head it or, heaven forbid, tackle an opponent.

The technique, if accompanied by copious, impassioned arm waving, shouting and gesticulating enables the more skilled practitioner to enjoy the game without having to involve himself directly in the play. This in turn increases the burden on the player's team-mates, who are obliged to redouble their efforts to compensate for the shortfall in numbers. As a result they quickly become knackered, so by the time they receive the ball their brains and limbs are so tired that they give it promptly back to the opposing team. The crowd is now duped into thinking that it's they who are inept and that our hero, in this case World Cup Willy, is the only one who can actually pass the ball, given that he alone isn't giving it away. What's more, the more experienced player is able to create the illusion that he's 'dying for the cause', 'busting a gut' or, best of all, 'running himself into the ground'.

Despite his relative inexperience, Barone, coached by Italy's best football minds, seemed to me pretty expert. With 20 minutes remaining and with the score at 0-3 he played his trump card. Running purposefully and quite quickly towards where the ball had recently been, he pulled up abruptly, clutched his hamstring, then keeled, theatrically and spectacularly, to the floor. Stretchered from the field well before the inevitable hissing, cat-calling and post-morteming began in earnest, Barone thus cleverly and convincingly evaded his not inconsiderable share of responsibility for Torino's spineless, woeful defeat. A classic footballing denouement. Or, if you will, a 'blinder'.

* * * *

And Sunday morning. Leaving the A26 motorway north of Lake Maggiore, 20 kilometers east of the Swiss border, we arrive this brisk, clear January day in yet another of the Italys. Villadossola, the desolate, putrefied chemical processing town of Germano Barale, one of Carpano's war horses, looks and feels like a place in retreat, huddled behind its myopia, afraid to emerge from its own filthy, corrosive shadow. Half-bred, ignored then orphaned, Villadossola has the air of a place which has long since given up whining for attention, given up pretending to love and be loved. This is a valley town, unlovable not in the way of the utilitarian, spoiled ski resorts of the Alps, for Villadossola had nothing spoiling, nothing to spoil. It's a great place for daydreamers, a great place for malingerers and layabouts and stoics. Come one come all, it's neither here nor there to Villadossola, it's past caring. The economic boom never reached this far north, couldn't be bothered with the place. This is a great place to sneak quietly away from...

You only need five minutes, three minutes in Germano Barale's company for the antidote. You can't not feel it, can't not see it when he speaks to you, *growls* to you. It never leaves them you see – men like him – can't ever leave them. It's latent. Latent and chemical. It's what they were, what they still are, absolutely without exception. They were born with it, blessed with it. The lucky ones, the truly stupid, got to learn, though never to understand, what it is, how to mine it. They learned to control it, mainly they learned to be controlled by it, to let it bully them and to dominate them. They learned to let it control and damage them, to wreck them. They learned how to get wrecked, became addicted to their bodies and to the rage and to the wrecking. Those hurt the most, the neediest, the most abandoned and least articulate, were the most blessed. Those with no interest in the dull, specious glory and insecurity of winning cycle races were the sport of professional cycling. Small, hungry, hard men with the weakest resistance to it, with neither the talent nor inclination for winning, the great unheard warriors of the road. The rest of life, the before and overwhelmingly the after was, is, by definition, just meaningless, colourless time wasting. A meagre, irrelevant fuck all. A half life. Fuck all. The rest of life is Villadossola.

And immediately you can see that he's a cyclist, see precisely the kind of cyclist he is, see that he means it. You can see the insatiable brutality of his work chiseled, scored into his face. Germano Barale's face has been *mapped*. His face looks like Paris–Roubaix, like a heinous, zigzagging Dolomite mountain. He looks like a cyclist, needs to talk to cycling people about cycling. He needs to talk a lot about cycling, to feel like a cyclist. How long have we got? He's 71 and has all of the time that's left. No, really, *all* of the time, though he knows it's not nearly enough. He talks like a man who's remembered how to breathe and it's an extraordinarily powerful, life affirming thing, a privilege to behold. He knows that for the most part I'm struggling to understand what he's saying and he couldn't care less and neither could I. He's got all these words to say and time's running out, and the more of the words he says the more he grows, the more like a man he becomes. The more he talks the more like Bartali and Anquetil and Nencini and Barale he feels. The more he talks the closer he gets to Balmamion, to Conterno and Bailetti, to Sartore. He knows that if he can just talk for long enough he'll find Germano Barale, the great *gregario* of Carpano. In truth, what he says is largely irrelevant, but it's imperative he says it, says all of it. How long have we got?

'Bordeaux-Gaul-Roubaix-Coppi-Giro-Bartali-Galibier-Balmamion-Liège-Bastogne-Liége-Nencini-Carpano-Giacotto.'

He's 23 again and rattling with the pills and the rage. And he has his strength, his mindless strength and his fast, strong bike, his tool. He's hungry and thirsty and immense and consumed and out of control. He's gasping for air and for water in the merciless humidity of the Pyrenees, thundering through the Forest of Arenberg, vindictive and electric with cold on a Dolomite descent, toe to toe with the ferocious Belgians at the Ronde, shaping the Giro with his colossal, frame-bending will. He's tachycardic again, like when Dr Peracino saved his life at the Tour (and what a day *that* was, how *strong* he was that day), a freight train smashing through Italy, smashing through Belgium and France and Switzerland and the thirst and the bullshit and the pain.

Germano ('Mano') Barale was born in Villadossola in 1936, the youngest of five brothers. Their Father kept a smallholding, 40 cows and a few sheep. To supplement the family income the boys would forage for and then sell firewood, making ends meet in their merciless, back-breaking world. Mano and his brother Giuseppe ('Pino'), two years older, were crazy for cycling but couldn't afford bikes. Salvation was found in the shape of the kindly Baldissera brothers. The Baldissera family had migrated west from Veneto, one of Northern Italy's very poorest regions, though quite why they chose Villadossola is anybody's guess. No matter, Veneto is a bulwark of Italian cycling and two of the Baldissera lads were keen riders. Following their own training ride, the brothers Baldissera would loan their disadvantaged neighbours a bike apiece and Mano and Pino would escape into the mountains, escape into their dreams, Coppi and Bartali for the afternoon. When, however, their neighbours upped sticks and returned to Veneto, the Barales found themselves once more without bikes and apparently without hope.

Pino Barale was a resourceful, self-assured teenager, independent and determined. Germano recalls the family inquest which took place the day he came home with an astonishing, brand new Stelvio bicycle, recalls his wonderment when he saw the Campagnolo gears, the abandonment he felt as his big brother sped off alone that afternoon. Family being family, the money was found and shy, tiny Mano was presented with his very own bike, his very own future. Now the boys trained together prodigiously. On the road they would see the best of the local amateur racers, guys they had read about in *La Gazzetta dello Sport*. They would studiously avoid contact for fear of making fools of themselves. Invited finally to join the chain gang the brothers acquitted themselves well, little Mano in particular impressing on the climbs. Funny and extrovert, he became the group mascot while his brother, the strong, silent type, gloried in the competitive element.

And the 'bike brothers' became good, seriously good riders. Soon they were beating all-comers in regional races and the cycling people of Piedmont began to take notice. In 1954, 19-year-old Pino Barale earned selection for the Italian Amateur Championship road race in Cosenza. There, 70 kilometers from the finish Pino, never one to hang around in a group, took off on the kind of madcap exploit which had served him well amongst the wanabees and also-rans in and around Osola. Incredibly he stayed away until Lino Grassi, a decent priced favourite and more than useful sprinter, jumped out from the peloton and caught him two kilometres from the line. What happened next is open to interpretation, but essentially Pino Barale won a two-man sprint to become national champion of Italy – a sprint Grassi has always claimed Barale had agreed to forgo. Grassi's version is that by the time he was caught Pino was so utterly stuffed that he implored him to take it easy. He would not contest the sprint in exchange for the dignity (and likely as not the professional contract to follow) of a close run thing, rather than the ignominy of being seen to run out of strength, to collapse in sight of the finish. Barale denied it but, notwithstanding his bravery and strength, and the wild party in Villadossola, mud sticks. Pino Barale was a fabulous rider but a questionable personality. He was an intransigent loner, the polar opposite of his kid brother. In 1956 Pino was selected to ride for Italy at the World Championships but refused to go without Mano, uncomfortable with the idea that he might be obliged to operate as part of a team.

The boys were frequent winners that season, Mano with 16 victories (he would have won a bucket load had he been able to sprint well), Pino with 20. The following year they signed professionally with Gino Bartali's San Pellegrino. Germano, who was completely awestruck by Bartali, remembers their first meeting:

'I was like a child. I referred to him as Mr Bartali, but he wasn't given to formality. He just said, "Enough of that nonsense, let's go to work."'

They went to work and Bartali quickly warmed to 'Baralino', less so to his older brother.

The 1957 Giro made a timely return to Osola after an absence of 28 years. With a single escapee down the road, the brothers Barale positioned themselves at the head of the peloton, driving it through their home town in the pouring rain, the entire region apparently at the roadside. Whilst Germano loved the donkey work of the *gregario* his brother, Pino, didn't take kindly to being told what to do – not by Bartali and not by anybody. No matter, the pair enjoyed decent results (Mano finished a creditable fourteenth at the Giro and came within an ace of winning the prestigious Giro di Veneto, crashing on the run-in) and were persuaded to sign for Fausto Coppi's reformed Bianchi team that winter. Established as pro bike racers, they were on their way.

At the Tour of Campania in southern Italy, Pino found himself in a five-man breakaway with the great Swiss rider Ferdi Kubler, one of Coppi's great rivals. From behind came the Bianchi team car with Mrs. Coppi aboard, instructing the youngster to slow and wait for Fausto, to use his immense strength not for himself but in the service of his captain. Pino told her to sling her hook in no uncertain terms, inviting her to 'tell Fausto to stay home if he doesn't have what it takes'. Five days later Bianchi announced their team for the Giro and only one Barale was selected. Pino Barale left cycling at the season's end, broken and disillusioned at only 23 years of age, his own worst enemy.

Mano carried on and would carry on carrying on, loved and respected by the entire peloton for his selflessness and unending good humour. Bruno Raschi, one of the more celebrated Italian sports journalists of the day, brilliantly wrote of Barale:

'He is the Gunga Din of the Giro, a truly great *gregario*. He is always faithful, a true guardian of his captain, like a soldier always ready to be first over the top. One has the impression that he would die for Defilippis, so readily does he absorb the pain and the suffering inherent in the work of the *gregario*. With the water he distributes comes bravery and charity, so happy is he in his brutal work. Among all of these conceited champions he is a shining example of what a cyclist could be, an angel of the road, renouncing himself in the service of the leaders he serves.'

Stories of Germano's generosity and humility are legion amongst those he worked with. One evening the Carpano riders found themselves billeted in a swanky San Remo hotel. The entertainment that night was provided by a popular, beautiful songstress of the time. Mano took courage and asked for her autograph, which was given. Giacotto, watching from afar, strode over and asked what the hell he was doing. Barale apologized and explained that he wanted an autograph for his wife. Giacotto was incensed.

'Never, ever ask people for an autograph, do you understand?' Germano apologized once more but explained that no, he didn't understand at all, what possible harm could it do?

'You are Germano Barale, do you not understand that? Do you not understand who you *are*? You are Germano Barale, the iron man of Carpano. She should be asking for *your* autograph!'

Then Giacotto fined him 50,000 lire.

One tale in particular seems apposite. Following Toni Bailetti's sheep-rustling exploit on stage four of the Giro and his own capture of the holiday at Ancona, Mano Barale offered Bailetti a trade – his fortnight's holiday by the seaside for Toni's livestock. When Bailetti refused on the basis that the Mano's holiday was of much greater value than his sheep, Barale insisted that he desperately needed more sheep and that Toni would be doing him a big favour. Bailetti, generous though somewhat bewildered, accepted and the deal was struck. When Giacotto got wind of it he politely enquired of Baralino why he'd done such shoddy business. Mano told him that he knew it was a bad deal but that he didn't care. Toni Bailetti was his friend. What's more he was about to get married and he would need a honeymoon.

Hearing these stories, listening to him speaking these words again, it's apparent that this Barale is a very, *very* hard little man, a *gregario* for one of cycling's great teams, fearsome and reckless in his loyalty, voracious in his altruism. Welcome to his world of humility and inhuman suffering, to the Giro d'Italia in the golden age of cycling. Welcome to a million miles from the facile, pampered world inhabited by today's professional sportsmen. Welcome to Mano Barale's world, a million miles from Villadossola.

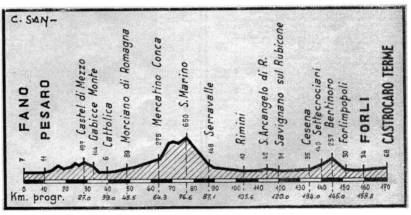

Stage 11

Stage eleven, 170 northerly kilometres to Castrocaro Terme, found the Giro routed through the picturesque hillside town of Bertinoro, home town of reigning champion Arnaldo Pambianco. In time honoured tradition the locals had a whip-round for an intermediate sprint prize, cobbling together the not inconsiderable sum of 100,000 lire. They did so in the hope that their favourite might manage to shake off his apparent lethargy and rediscover the form of the previous May. Then he had earned himself the pink jersey by joining the right break on a flat stage to Florence, before holding off Gaul and Anquetil with an heroic eleven-hour performance over 275 snow covered kilometres on the terrible, mythical Passo Stelvio.

A nice idea then, but misguided: Pambianco's form this year was lousy. There was no way he could win the 1962 Giro and he would never again finish in the top ten. By the time the race sped through disappointed Bertinoro with 25 kilometres remaining he was already well off the pace. Up front Vittorio Adorni, now an elegant second-year professional earmarked for stardom, piloted a strong seven-man breakaway with a powerful attack on the climb to San Marino. Guido Neri, born and raised only a half dozen kilometres from the stage finish, was given permission to try his hand, whilst another local boy, Diego Ronchini, anxious not only to win on home soil but to improve his chances overall, also made the split. Depressingly for these three and their fellow escapees, they found themselves in the company not only of Faema's Zilverberg but also the world's greatest finisher, Rik Van Looy. No contest. Van Looy sprinted imperiously to victory as the Belgian team continued to mock the Giro with a fifth stage-win. The peloton rolled in two minutes in arrears minus young Meco, laid low by a hunger flat. Out of fuel and out of luck, the lesser spotted Abruzzese conceded eight minutes and the dream of a podium finish at his first Giro.

*Stage 12: Bruno Meali crosses the line ahead of Willy Schroeders,
who is already beginning to make his protest.*

STAGE TWELVE

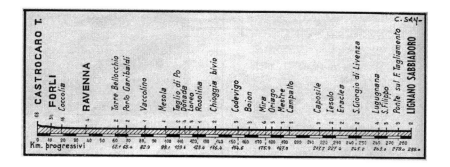

On Wednesday 30th May the Giro continued its meander north along the Adriatic coastline for stage twelve, at 298 kilometres the longest of the race. The stage concluded at another of Folchi's 'touristic sensations', the dreary seaside resort of Lignano Sabbiadoro, neatly sandwiched between Venice and well to do Trieste. These transition stages, baking hot, overlong and pan flat, are invariably the dog days of the grand tours, and this was no exception. For 200 kilometres the peloton, mindful of the severity of the final week ahead, simply dithered along marking time, hour after soporific hour of it. The occasional rider popping out here and there to greet loved ones on the roadside, a broken collarbone for young Casati (he'd find no sympathy today; what kind of pillock crashes at 30kph?), from time to time a minor mechanical problem. A nice relaxed lunch at Rosolina in the early afternoon sunshine, old friends and new breaking bread in the peloton. The awestruck, flag-waving children of gleeful coastal villages resplendent for the day in the pink of the Giro. In scorching Caprile ice-cream and wildly exaggerated tales of the great champions Coppi, Binda and Girardengo. Picnics in Ghirlo, red wine and sunstroke on the picturesque little beach at Mira. Out on the road the odd young gun naïvely, needlessly disturbing the equilibrium by attempting an *exploit*, brought sharply to heel by Van Looy's snarling, pockmarked northern sentries. No alarms and no surprises then, but a pleasant day's cyclotourism – agreeable, civilized and, in the context of the race, totally irrelevant, utterly pointless.

Six meaningless hours in, at Marghera on the grimy, industrial outskirts of Venice, a group of seven rebels led by the Molteni pair, De Rosso and Fornoni, finally remembered they were participants in a bike-race and began to race their bikes. The strike breakers, GC deadbeats to a man, took fully 11 minutes in only 60 kilometres before settling to the peculiar cat and mouse, attack and counter-attack business that always distinguishes the final 20 kilometres on days like these. Despite the best efforts of the two Moltenis and the Basque rider, Salvador, the fugitives hit the finishing straight together, leaving the fast finishing Bruno Mealli of the Moschettieri and Willy Schroeders to fight it out, almost literally, at the death.

Mealli it was who heaved himself over the line first, leaving Schroeders, shouting, gesticulating, finger pointing, apoplectic. Complaining bitterly (and correctly) that the young Tuscan had baulked his man, Faema's *Directeur Sportif,* Lomme Driessens, the archetypal Flemish riot in a phone box rabble-rouser, launched an immediate appeal. At long last some entertainment.

Italians, particularly Italians in official blazers, love nothing more than a dramatic, pretentious, self-important farce. Place your bets folk, this *fait accompli* could go either way.

Surprisingly, and it must be said magnanimously, the Italian jury concurred with Driessens that the Italian rider had deviated wildly and dangerously from his line. They fined him 10,000 lire and warned him not to do it again. Schroeders, for his troubles and for 'removing his hands from the bars in the last 150 metres of the stage' received a rebuke of his own. And a fine – 20,000 lire.

And the stage was awarded to? Mealli or Schroeders? Italian or Dutch? I'll leave you take a wild guess.

WOULD THE REAL CHAMPION PLEASE STAND UP?

Bruno Mealli would find himself cast unwittingly as a pawn in a *genuine* Giro controversy, one of truly seismic proportions, in 1963. In April Mealli had finished second behind the popular Venetian, Marino Fontana, in the Italian National Championship. Fontana thus earned for one year the prestige of the traditional red, white and green tricoloured jersey of the Champion. Later, Adriano Rondoni, President of the UVI, the Italian cycling federation, received notification that Fontana had been the beneficiary of an illicit wheel change *en route*; Fontana was promptly stripped of the Championship and *maglia tricolore*, and Mealli declared the Champion.

Fontana and his team were appalled, and with good reason. Cyclists had traded wheels (in addition to food, drugs, alcohol, races, contracts and so on...) with impunity for decades – it was an accepted if technically illegal practice of the road – so why the stink now, if not for political point-scoring? He appealed to the League of Professional Cyclists who found overwhelmingly in his favour, thereby creating a schism at the top of cycling with both sides – loosely speaking the management and the trade union of the sport – declaring the sovereignty of governance. As the row intensified the Federation and the League became ever more entrenched in their respective positions, leaving two humble bike riders unwittingly embroiled in a bitter struggle for the control of the sport. Mealli, a hard-working, popular and above average rider, became an outcast through no fault of his own. Ordered by both the UVI (in consultation with the UCI, the international governing body of the sport) and the management of his Cynar team to wear a jersey he and his peers knew he'd neither earned nor deserved, the Tuscan found himself in an invidious position – damned if he wore the jersey; fired if he didn't. Meanwhile Fontana and his team, Gino Bartali's San Pellegrino, fully and very vocally supported by the peloton, launched a further appeal to CONI, the Italian Olympic committee. CONI, priggish and demure, sided with the Federation, rendering Fontana's *tricolore*, and by implication the League of Professional cyclists, illegal.

So, on 19th May, the 46th Giro departed Naples with the hapless Mealli in the national champion's jersey, Fontana in the standard issue orange of San Pellegrino. All well and good? Problem solved? Not entirely. Six kilometres into the race Fontana stripped off his team jersey to reveal – you guessed it – a *maglia tricolore*, much to the amusement of the peloton, the mortified embarrassment of both the Giro and the UVI. This was the very first Giro to be televised live as Italy's state broadcaster RAI showed the last 10 kilometres of the stages during an hour long show called 'Processo alla Tappa', presented by the legendary Adriano De Zan.*

Though deeply injurious to the credibility of the race, the whole sordid spectacle sprinkled journalistic gold dust on the fledgling television 'show'. The producers were able to focus not only on the great rivalries set to play themselves out over the ensuing three weeks, but also on this gripping, if unedifying subplot; a more than useful diversion during the often flat, often dull stages of the opening week of the Giro. The show thus had its first major coup, not only in securing interviews with both Fontana and the ever popular Bartali, but also the journalistic hijacking of a tongue-tied Mealli by RAI's roving reporters.

That evening the UVI met with the official UCI appointed race jury in Potenza and requested that Fontana leave the Giro, upon which the League of Professional Cyclists, now under legal counsel, made a proclamation of its own: the jury had no authority over the professional peloton, and Fontana would continue to race. Following a night of infantile to-ing and fro-ing the morning of stage two dawned with the two parties still more intractable. First the jury reiterated its position: if Fontana took the start line the jury would abandon the race, rendering the Giro illegal, unsanctioned and outlawed by the UCI, governing body of all professional racing. An hour before the scheduled stage roll-out the League, in the form of the directors of the twelve Giro teams, held a last-gasp summit of their own. Fearful of the contractual and legal ramifications of a no-show at the showpiece event of the season, the teams met, prophetically enough, in the Broomwagon, the bus which travels behind the peloton to pick up those riders unable to complete the day's racing and to signify the conclusion of the race caravan. The Giro version of the Broomwagon carried the legend *Fine della corsa*,

---

* Thirty years later, when RAI lost the rights to broadcast the Giro, outbid by Silvio Berlusconi's Fininvest corporation, De Zan was replaced as programme anchor by his own son Davide. De Zan Senior died of leukaemia in 2001, aged only 69, but Davide has become one of Italian cycling's more reasoned, more authoritative journalists through the slew of doping scandals to have beset the sport over the last decade.

literally 'End of the race', an irony lost on nobody, with the race (and RAI's great televisual creation) appearing all but stillborn.

Now the League, under threat of heavy sanctions from *La Gazzetta dello Sport* and their sponsors, gambled that the jury dare not turn its back on the Giro; they decided to ride and be damned. Fontana, and the stage, would start with or without UVI approval. With the patronage of professional sport the subject of an embarrassing televisual squabble, the row found its way into parliament, with the Giro itself famously and melodramatically declared illegal. Given that the riders, managers, race organizers, UVI, UCI, jury, League and their respective lawyers were now technically all fugitives from the various arcane by-laws being invoked, no less a figure than Antonio Segni, the new President of the Republic of Italy, stepped purposefully into the breach. Upon receipt of a begging telegram from the various journalists associated with the race imploring him to 'consider the fatal consequences the suspension of the Giro could have, not only for cycling, but for all of professional sport in Italy', Segni rushed a bill through parliament in favour of CONI. And very obviously nobody took a blind bit of notice.

Actually not quite nobody. Rik Van Looy, the Emporer of Herentals, wasn't about to be pushed around by a two-bob despot like Segni. Van Looy took his considerable appearance fees, declared the Republic of Italy officially illegal and promptly buggered off home to Belgium, as did the rest of his team.

Following a further five days of acrimonious bickering, a heartbroken Fontana slipped away from the race. Then the management of San Pellegrino withdrew from the Giro, and from cycle sport, effectively abandoning a team of riders and support staff, not to mention their wives and families, to their fate. Most of them, notably the GC favourites Zancanaro and Aldo Moser, had little choice but to ride on in the hope of earning some money. Wearing a plain black jersey bearing the moniker '11 sport' – the number 11 indicative of their position as the eleventh and final team in the race – they continued. Zancanaro, in particular, excelled against the odds, winning a stage and a podium finish in Milan. Funny old game.

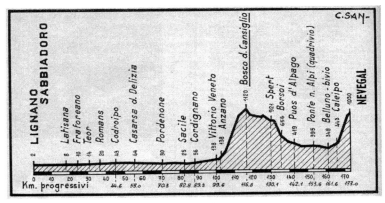

Stage 13

Armand Desmet and Rik Van Looy

STAGE THIRTEEN

The 1962 edition of the Giro d'Italia finally turned left and inland for the promised land of the Dolomite Mountains on day 13, the stage culminating in a 10-kilometre climb to the ski station of Nevegal. Here Defilippis made his move, attacking mid-stage over the biggest climb of the day, the Bosco. By the summit Nino had almost two minutes over the peloton as the stricken Pambianco became the first of the big favourites to fall by the wayside, losing contact as the road began to rise. He would abandon that evening with stomach trouble. Though doubtless spectacular, Nino's 60-kilometre bid for glory was premature and ultimately futile, as he found himself reeled in 30 kilometres from the finish. On the climb to Nevegal the 1962 Giro finally began to reveal itself, as a group of four containing Guido 'Coppino' Carlesi broke free. By his own admission Carlesi, second in the Tour de France the previous year, had arrived in Milan short of fitness; in view of the mountainous route Coppino had decided to ride the Giro as training for the Tour, less hilly and in theory better suited to his racing style (a big mistake, as he would finish a lowly 19th in France and would never again come remotely close to winning there). Here though he excelled, winning a two-up sprint with the climber *par excellence,* Angelino Soler, to claim an unlikely stage-win as the GC contenders, specifically Massignan, Gaul and Taccone, began their Giro in earnest.

First to cross amongst the favourites was the *maglia rosa* Desmet, just seven seconds down. Elsewhere, Gaul surprisingly ceded 30 seconds to sixth placed Massignan, while Taccone cracked horribly, surrendering over four minutes. Defilippis and Balmamion, finishing in a group containing, amongst others, Graziano Battistini, each lost just over a minute. A creditable if unremarkable showing from Carpano, a wake up call for the lacklustre Gaul, a near catastrophe for Taccone. Time for the real Giro to stand up.

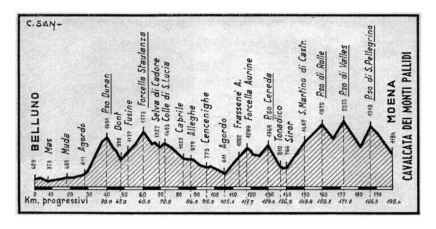

On Friday 1st June, 110 anxious, distracted riders took a rest day at Nevegal in the shadow of the giant Marmolada, the highest peak in the great mountain range. Ahead lay the most percussive of all stages, a 198-kilometre climbing marathon to incorporate no fewer than seven big Dolomite passes. First the Passo Duran, 10 kilometres of ascent on a dirt road to an altitude of 1,600m, followed by another unpaved 10-kilometre grind to the Forcella Staulanza at 1,773 metres. Next, across the valley to the Forcella Aurine for a further 12 kilometres of climbing before a short, dangerous descent to the Passo di Cereda, essentially a track, just about passable with favourable weather and good tyres. The legendary Rolle (amongst the first great Dolomite passes to be included in the Giro, back in 1937), a torturous 20-kilometre ramp to 1,970 metres, would precede the awful Valles, at 2,033 metres the high point of the Giro, and finally the Passo San Pellegrino, a viciously steep 6-kilometre brute of a climb, again on 'beaten earth'.

The blond, close-cropped West Flandrian all-rounder, Armand Desmet, runner up at the 1960 Tour of Spain, held the *maglia rosa*. At 31, Desmet, a tough-as-teak rider in the best Flemish tradition, had arrived at the Giro in the best form of his life. In March he'd finished a creditable third in his home race, the prestigious mid-week cobbled classic Ghent–Wevelgem, before cementing his form in riding to fourth at the Paris–Nice, performing well in support of team-mate and overall winner, Jo Planckaert. He confirmed his excellence in soloing to victory as Faema dominated Germany's premiere single-day marathon, Henninger Turm, a week in advance of the Giro. Here, given free reign by the team to attack the General Classification following Rik Van Looy's capitulation on stage five, Desmet had once more exceeded expectations with his outstanding climbing. At best unfancied, but in the main ignored before the race, Desmet now harboured genuine and apparently well founded ambitions of retaining the jersey once the real suffering began. Furthermore, and contrary to the Giro organisers' best-laid plans, foreign riders occupied five of the top six positions with the classy Anglade, previously a Tour de France runner up, riding ominously well in second place. The dangerous Spaniards, Suarez and Pérez-Francés, useful climbers both, lay third and sixth respectively. Of the pre-race favourites, Graziano Battistini stood fourth at 5'09", Massignan seventh at 6'16", a strangely subdued Charly Gaul eleventh at 6'42". Nino Defilippis at 7'29" lay tenth with his rallying team-mate, Franco Balmamion, a further six minutes adrift. Though effectively out of contention for the leader's jersey, the Canavese, on paper the best of Carpano's climbers, now fancied his chances of a high overall placing.

That evening, as Balmamion's team-mates once more entertained the idea that their young eagle might yet soar in the rarefied atmosphere of the mountains, Giacotto ruminated on how best to convince an increasingly truculent Defilippis that he might wish to contemplate for a second time a joint leadership role.

In the early hours of Sunday 2nd June, as the peloton slept its uneasy sleep, race Director Vincenzo Torriani was given word that an apocalyptic weather front threatened to wreck its way into the mountains. Torriani, a man with a heightened sense of history and of drama, had overseen epic Dolomite stages before, notably Gaul's race-winning nine-hour battle through precisely these weather conditions in 1956. As an ominous black fog descended over breakfast Torriani decreed the race would go ahead.

With the weather closing in over the Duran climb the peloton huddled together, the better to keep morale up, the freeze at bay. Meanwhile, little Angelino Soler, brave as a lion and keen to increase his lead in the Mountains competition, plugged on ahead. Following a treacherous descent in poor visibility it began to snow. As the riders, barely able to control their bikes so frozen were their hands, began their ascent of the Forcella Staulanza, a leading group of 12 formed, amongst them Desmet, Baldini, Balmamion, Battistini, the Frenchman Anglade and the stylish Spaniard Pérez-Francés.

Here the peloton began the wholesale abandonment of the Giro. Walter Martin recalls the scene:

'I can't remember much, just the extreme cold. I felt that everything was out of control. There were abandoned bikes everywhere, riders walking, running, falling over as the snow turned to ice, shouting for help, deranged. I was absolutely frozen. In the end I just couldn't do it any more. I felt like my body was shutting down. I climbed into the broomwagon. I was wrecked.'

The Angel of the Mountains himself, Gaul, was amongst the first to climb from his bike. Gambling on the annulment of the stage, Gaul calculated that if enough riders stopped the organisers would be left with no option but to call the whole thing off. Then Van Looy, tired of the cold, of Italian jingoism, and of Gino Bartali in particular, invited his Faema team-mates to do likewise. All but Desmet and Huub Zilverberg gleefully accepted. Bartali, Sporting Director of San Pellegrino, was no great lover of the autocratic Van Looy, self-styled 'Emporer' of Belgium cycling. Bartali believed that Van Looy's revolutionary tactic of deploying his team, the so-called 'Red Guard', to pilot him to within 300 yards of the finish line, from whence he invariably won comfortably, so superior was his sprint, was morally reprehensible, entirely outside the spirit of cycling. Gino the pious neglected to mention that Van Looy was eminently capable of winning *any* race on *any* terrain, team or no team, and in theory capable of winning the Giro, a state of affairs both he and the organisers were to keen to avoid in the light of the recent spate of foreign victors. Bartali embarked on a tiresome campaign, encouraged by and played out in the media, of urging the home-based teams to combine against Faema in particular, but also the French Liberia–Grammont team led by the impressive Anglade.

Gaul, normally one of the smartest, most calculating minds in the peloton, badly misunderstood the mood of the times. Given that neither the race organisers nor the Italian public wanted to see another foreigner carry the *maglia rosa* into Milan, his abandonment effectively ensured that, no matter how atrocious the conditions, the stage result would stand. The overwhelming favourite for the Giro was out of the race, his bluff called on a stage apparently tailor-made for his assault on the general classification.

Over the summit of the Forcella Staulanza Balmamion, the only Carpano in the lead group, found a frantic, gesticulating Vincenzo Giacotto stood beside his own (private) car. The bewildered Canavese was ordered to stop and change into dry, warm team kit. On the descent he punctured, repaired it himself as best he could, then waited fully four minutes for the Amiraglia, a replacement wheel and second Carpano wave. A frozen Defilippis had climbed off on the descent of the Duran before remounting under persuasion from Conterno and Barale, Carpano's human bulldozers. Barale hadn't been prepared to let his captain surrender:

'The leaders had a job to do, just as we *gregari* did. If Nino had abandoned it would have cost us money. If I had to survive then so did he. We reminded him of his responsibilities and persuaded him to get back on the bike.'

More chaff bailed out on the descent before the remaining hard cases of the peloton, buoyed by the slightly improved weather conditions they found in the valley, began the 40-kilometre slog to the foot of the Aurine, at 12 kilometres nominally the easiest of the climbs, an average 6% gradient included here to soften up the riders in advance of the real hurt. Meanwhile, those journalists who had driven the course ahead of the race had the Chief of Police contact Covolo, President of the League of Professional Cyclists. Unbeknownst to the stalwart Torriani and the lion hearts now bracing themselves under renewed snowfall for the Aurine, the Valles and San Pellegrino passes were already impassable under several inches of snow. Covolo, thus informed of the devastation threatening every rider on every descent, continued to vacillate. Still no call to Torriani, still more riders climbing off, still the weather ridiculing the survivors, still Carpano chasing, frantic to save the Giro.

Now the *maglia rosa* Desmet, hard-as-hell Flemish, first crashed, then punctured, crashed again, collapsed. He would lose 18 minutes, a futile, heroic catastrophe. At the front a group of 16 formed, minus Soler, his mountains points won, still minus Defilippis and Balmamion, allies *in extremis*. As Vincenzo Meco galloped clear of the leaders, anxious to put one over on his fellow Abruzzese Taccone, more frozen souls succumbed to the professional cyclists' worst enemy – self preservation

– and capsized into the abject, miserable warmth of the ambulance and of their team cars.

At the summit Meco and his shadow, Julio San Emeterio of Ferrys, led by almost two minutes. Another descent in thick fog, the snow replaced by freezing, pelting rain; a hideous lottery for the brave, the reckless and the stupid. Bravest and stupidest by far was Balmamion. As Angelo Conterno's resolve evaporated, he brilliantly towed Defilippis and Barale up the Passo Cereda, bridging across to the leaders on the descent as Battistini assumed the virtual *maglia rosa*. Now Covolo got word to Torriani: it was still snowing on the Rolle, the descent almost completely blocked by snow.

Vincenzo Meco on the Rolle

As the blizzard intensified, with riders still falling and climbing off all over the road and team cars abandoned for lack of traction, the race as a spectacle seemed in imminent danger of imploding. Three kilometres from the summit Torriani finally called merciful time on proceedings, announcing that the stage would end at the top of the mountain, 38 kilometres and two big climbs short of the official finish. Now poor San Emeterio suffered a flat tyre, affording young Meco a famous though slightly pyrrhic victory. Three minutes later the cream of the race – Baldini, Massignan, Defilippis, Battistini, Taccone and Pérez-Francés – grovelled to the top together with Balmamion, Carpano's king for the day, a further 40 seconds back. Beneath him chaos, torment and devastation as the organizers prayed enough would survive to allow the continuation of the Giro.

Barale remembers his experiences on the Rolle:

'It was horrific. I stopped three times. Doctor Peracino told me to get as much sugar as I could so every time I saw a bar I ran in, stole all the chocolate and demanded Cognac. When we got back to the hotel in Moena I just collapsed on my bed and tried to sleep. It was hopeless, though, because my body had gone into shock from the cold, the exhaustion, the sugar and the Cognac. I was delirious. They tried to get me down for dinner but I refused to move. I was too tired to get out of the bed, never mind think about walking to the dining room. I remember being in the bed and feeling neurotic, terrified that if I had to get up the cold would start again. So I never ate that night – I knew the consequences would be awful for me later, but I felt completely crippled, emotionally and physically. It was the hardest day I ever had on a bike, probably one of the worst days I ever had in my life.'

The following morning Defilippis, with typical hubris, claimed he'd been about to launch an attack when Torriani pulled the plug. Regardless, Battistini once more led the Giro by three seconds from Anglade, with Pérez-Francés third at 31 seconds. Massignan lay fourth, Defilippis fifth some 2'20" behind the leader, Taccone tenth at 7'22". Balmamion had fought his way back up to a respectable eleventh at 8'49":

'To be honest I quite enjoyed the stage. I decided not to go too deep on the Rolle because I'd towed Nino for nearly 80 kilometres and I knew the stage would have big consequences in the days ahead. I was feeling strong, like the Giro was beginning again for me.'

Poor, pitiable Armand Desmet, carried frozen by a mechanic from his bike to the team car, had capitulated to thirteenth. Forty-five years on, older and wiser, the Flandrian remains frustrated by his team's ineptitude and their readiness to throw in the towel:

'I rode the entire stage without a rain jacket, just a soaking wet short sleeved pink jersey. Driessens, the *Directeur Sportif*, had forgotten to bring them – to the Dolomites! What's more there's no way they would've abandoned if Van Looy had been in the pink jersey.'

As for Torriani, his munificence in curtailing proceedings early was immediately seen precisely for what it was – an exercise in self-preservation, albeit a race-saving one. In all the stage saw 56 riders abandon, amongst them three from Carpano – Kurt Gimmi, Walter Martin and Ernesto Minetto. A total of 54 survived what the Torinese daily *La Stampa* would describe as 'the most horrific scene in the history of cycling'. Toni Bailetti reckons that no more than 20 actually rode to the finish, the rest were ferried in by team cars as the organizers turned a conveniently blind eye.

And so the 45th Giro d'Italia staggered on.

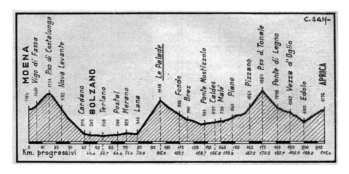

Stage 15

STAGE FIFTEEN

Stage fifteen, 215 kilometres from the picturesque wooden chalet village of Moena to Aprica, was billed as the second Dolomite climbing festival and, quite appropriately, given the prestigious third Sunday slot. The first climb, the relatively easy 9-kilometre Costalunga, would precede a long descent into lazy, affluent, Germanic (architecturally and linguistically if not culturally) Bolzano, the capital of Italian South Tyrol. Then the Passo Palade, in truth a fairly monotonous uphill slog of seventeen kilometres, before the legendary Tonale, one of the first of the Dolomite climbs to be tackled by the great Giro pioneers all those years previously.

Amongst the leaders a predictable truce was observed over the first two climbs, the pain of the day before nailed hard into shattered legs. Then, with the peloton contemplating the feed, 80 kilometres from the finish at the tiny village of Male, young Vittorio Adorni, 17th overall and almost 13 minutes behind Battistini, gambled his lunch for a slice of Giro glory and won, brilliantly. Crossing the line in bright sunshine seven minutes before the Battistini group, Adorni served notice on a sparkling career and climbed to eighth place overall. Five kilometres from the top of the Tonale, with the stage in danger of becoming a GC non-event, Vito Taccone finally broke ranks. Over the top and up the long drag to the finish he put three minutes into the leaders, impressively hauling himself back into contention as Anglade, complaining of stomach cramps, lost upwards of three minutes to the *maglia rosa* group, thereby severely compromising his Giro challenge. Although the stage ultimately proved inconclusive, Balmamion, finishing with the stupendously strong Germano Barale, comfortably amongst the elite of the race, benefited as Guido Carlesi's form deserted him. Balmamion thus climbed, for the first time, into the top ten – a notable recovery and a job well done.

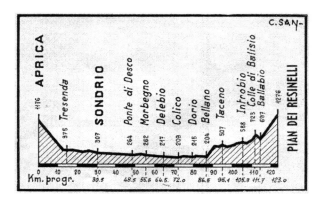

The final Dolomite stage, the 16th, rolled west out of the Ski station of Aprica towards the great Lakes of Lombardia, the spiritual home of Italian cycling. Still today the area remains the command post of the sport in the Peninsula, a magnet for aspiring cyclists from all corners of Europe. To ride out of Milan or Bergamo on a crisp spring morning is to feel a profound sense of the history and fellowship imbued by over a century of shared experiences. In Lombardia more than anywhere else in Europe one feels cycling lore hewn into the landscape, as thousands escape the urban sprawl for the sharp, breathable air of the hills and the great lakes of Como and Lecco, riding in the shadows of Magni, Gimondi and Motta.

Today's stage, short at only 123 kilometres, would conclude with a beautiful mountain top *denouement* at Pian dei Resinelli, 1,300m above Lake Lecco. The climb, though only eight kilometres in length, was hurtful in its severity, designed to re-configure the general classification before the following day's transitional run towards the Piedmontese Alps.

Early in the stage an unknown Tuscan neo-pro named Graziano Corsini, from San Pellegrino, escaped alone. With the leaders pensively eyeing one another, 35 kilometres from the finish, Soler launched his now customary attack on a short, punchy little climb, the Colle di Balisio. Balmamion, better with each passing day but apparently still no great shakes on GC, cleverly jumped on the Spaniard's back wheel, as did the Swiss, Freddy Ruegg. Ten kilometres later, with poor Corsini caught and dropped, the peloton lay two minutes adrift as Soler inexorably increased the heat. Recognising that Soler was untouchable, Balmamion calmly rode the final climb at tempo, dropping Ruegg to claim second on the stage, 1'27" behind the winner. Three minutes later Meco arrived with (of all people) Armand Desmet, battered but unbroken. Then came Vito Taccone, preceding Battistini, Pérez-Francés, Defilippis *et al* by a useful 53 seconds. Biggest loser of the day was the stricken Anglade. The Frenchman conceded another four minutes to Battistini and would abandon the next day. Notwithstanding Defilippis' wild, and wildly inaccurate, accusations of betrayal (Giacotto had given Balmamion permission to ride as he saw fit), Balmamion climbed to an unlikely seventh place.

With five stages remaining the General Classification stood as follows:

1. Graziano Battistini	Legnano	92hr 22'31"
2. Jose Pérez-Francés	Ferry's	@ 31"
3. Imerio Massignan	Legnano	@1'18"
4. Nino Defilippis	Carpano	@2'20"
5. Vito Taccone	Atala	@3'17"
6. Ercole Baldini	Moschettieri	@3'42"
7. Franco Balmamion	Carpano	@4'23"
11. Armand Desmet	Faema	@8'49"

Of 130 starters only 54 remained in the race. It is instructive to have an understanding of the relative strength of the leaders' teams. The diluted Peloton broke down as follows:

Legnano	7 riders
Ferry's	2 riders
Carpano	7 riders
Atala	4 riders
Moschettieri	6 riders

For Legnano, Battistini, a Tour de France runner-up recently turned 26, was approaching his prime as a cyclist. Strong, experienced and tactically accomplished, he continued to justify his position among the pre-race favourites. His team-mate Massignan, a year younger, was a pure climber, ideally suited and well placed to wrestle the initiative in the Alps should Battistini falter. In addition, Legnano retained five *gregari* and an experienced manager in Eberado Pavesi. With two exceptional leaders, Legnano appeared in an excellent position to carry off the big prize, particularly in the light of the poisonous atmosphere now enveloping Carpano.

Defilippis, marginalised by what he perceived as Giacotto's lack of faith and increasingly alienated from his team-mates, began to rail against the resurgent Balmamion. Conveniently overlooking the fact that the youngster had at all times ridden entirely according to team orders, Nino sought to impugn Franco's character, both within the team and to an incredulous media. Balmamion, to his eternal credit, refused to be drawn, in part because he held Defilippis in high regard and saw no value in inflaming an already difficult situation, but principally because he felt desperately uncomfortable with a microphone shoved up his nose. He simply put his head down and rode. History (and the prevailing consensus around the race) suggested that Defilippis would in all probability crack in the high mountains, in which case Balmamion might sneak into the top five.

The elegant Spaniard Pérez-Francés, though a consistently high-class performer, would struggle to survive with no support. For the expensively assembled Moschettieri, with Pambianco long since retired and Nencini 16 minutes in arrears, the Giro was a near shambles, mitigated only slightly by the publicity value of Baldini's improvement and a couple of stage-wins, one highly contentious, by the seaside. In the unlikely event that a threat would emerge to the Legnano hegemony, the enigmatic Taccone looked the man most likely, though with limited support the likelihood of his overhauling both Battistini *and* Massignan appeared remote at best.

Second over the line at Pian dei Resinelli on Stage 16

FRANCO AND NINO

Beyond the *maglia rosa* the *maglia tricolore* – the red, white and green jersey of the National Champion – is the most prestigious in Italian cycling. In 1962 the championship had been won courageously by Nino Defilippis. Over three single-day races held in April he demonstrated his all round excellence to claim the jersey for a second time. First he defeated Ronchini and Carlesi in a three-up sprint to win the Tour of Lazio in Rome, before Carlesi triumphed in the Tour of Tuscany, with Nino beaten into sixth. At the Tour of Piedmont Defilippis, advised by Peracino not to race due to chronic headache – 'I had to be helped onto my bike; I literally couldn't stand up' – finished tenth, well ahead of Carlesi and Ronchini, to claim the jersey.

Bizarrely, on the morning of Wednesday 5th June, he fetched up at the start line wearing not the *tricolore* but a standard issue black and white Carpano team jersey, much to the bewilderment of Giacotto, his team-mates and presumably everyone else associated with the race. The race jury, incensed by Defilippis' flagrant lack of respect for protocol and tradition, promptly issued a 10,000 lire fine, derisory but symbolic.

Quite why Nino chose this day to not wear the jersey he'd worked so hard for and of which he was apparently immensely proud remains something of a moot point within the Torinese cycling community. Nino has subsequently claimed that he wore the team issue jersey in the hope that Legnano might confuse him for a *gregario* and unwittingly allow him the freedom to escape. This seems fanciful in the extreme, for a number of reasons. With the possible exceptions of Baldini and Nencini, Defilippis was the best, and best known, cyclist in Italy. Quick witted, intelligent and opinionated, Defilippis was popular with supporters and journalists alike. In addition, he was the Champion of Italy, lay fourth in the Giro and stood a decent outside chance of winning it. He was Nino Defilippis and he was news. The notion that he might be able to arrive at the start with hundreds of supporters, journalists, team personnel and race officials present, register to ride and then 'hide' from Battistini and Massignan in a peloton of only 54 riders is absurd, probably the more so *just because* he was wearing the wrong jersey.

The background to Defilippis' behaviour, and to his uncharacteristic antipathy towards Balmamion, is complex but worthy of examination. Nino is by nature a kindly man, effusive and eager to please. When I arrived unannounced at his restaurant he immediately downed tools, dashed home and later returned with a signed copy of his autobiography. He then insisted that Mecu and I join him for lunch on the house and put himself at my disposal for a round of facile questions, throughout which he was unstintingly polite and candid. What then were the circumstances predicating his peculiar behaviour on the morning of 5th June 1962? Where, in the vernacular, was Nino's head?

Professional cyclists of the modern era tend to race a maximum of 70 days a year. They carefully select the races in which they want to be competitive, typically no more than 40 days in any given season, and use the remainder to augment scientifically prepared training programmes, with a huge emphasis placed on rest and recuperation. Team rosters are generally large, often in excess of 30 riders segmented into three or four separate 'cells' of ten or so; one cell might train for and concentrate on the Tour de France, a second unit will ride the Giro and the Vuelta, another will specialize in the early season Northern Classics and the smaller stage races. These factors, allied to advancements in bike manufacturing, an improved understanding of nutrition, biomechanical testing and much shorter, less demanding races, enable the better riders to remain competitive, often until their mid-30s, occasionally beyond. In the 1950s and early 1960s, when Nino was at the peak of his powers, the lot of a top cyclist was infinitely more demanding. Teams were small, with typically no more than 13 to 15 riders. They rode most if not all of the races for which they received an invitation from mid-February to October, then indoors on the track through the winter months.

To take one example, in 1956 alone Nino completed a full early season classics programme, including Milan–San Remo, Milan–Torino, the Tour of Piedmont and a host of others, before riding the 17 stages of the Vuelta a España between 26th April and 11th May. Here he won a stage and the King of the Mountains prize, defeating no lesser figure than Federico Bahamontes, the great climber dubbed the 'Eagle of Toledo'. Nino then took part in a series of criterium races in Spain, before arriving once more in Milan for the start of the Giro on 19th May. He abandoned the race on stage 18, in the blizzard which saw Gaul claim his epic victory. Following a further round of Criteriums, Defilippis rode a five-day stage race in France before proceeding to the Tour with one aim. The race crossed the Alps into Piedmont that year, with a stage finish in Turin's Stadio Comunale, the shared home of 'Juve' and 'Toro'. This was to be Nino's big day. He won stages in Pau and Toulouse before superbly outsprinting everyone in the Comunale. 'It was absolutely full, like for the Turin Derby. An unforgettable day, one of the best of my career.' He would finish fifth overall, as the unknown Frenchman, Roger Walkowiak, produced a virtual carbon copy of Clerici's Giro coup of 1954. He estimates that in the course of that year he rode competitively over 200 times – an astonishing, though by no means unique, workload.

The 1962 Giro, at 4,180 kilometres some 735 longer than the 2005 edition, included no less than eight stages for which the winners' finishing time exceeded six and a half hours. The longest stage in 2005, over 223 kilometres, took six hours and one minute to complete; in 1962 Bruno Mealli spent eight and a half hours in the saddle in winning the 298-kilometre 12th stage, one of the three to have exceeded eight hours. Little wonder then that, at only 30 years of age, Nino was fast approaching the end of his illustrious career, the majority of his contemporaries completely washed up, so physically ruinous was a life in cycling.

In addition to the Flanders debacle, Nino had suffered a further devastating defeat in 1961, narrowly beaten into second place at the World Championship road race by Rik Van Looy. Keen to establish his primacy and influence among a fresh intake of young riders at a restructured Carpano, he had ridden well throughout the spring of 1962, evidenced by his win at the Tour of Lazio and capture of the *tricolore*. He was in form and motivated for the Giro, confident of winning some stages.

Though they grew up less than 30 kilometres apart, Balmamion and Defilippis are, in outlook and temperament, as different as night and day. As we have discovered, Franco was brought up in the heart of the 'Copperlands' of the Lanzo Valley, in the lee of the great Alps. The area is known for its metalworking tradition, its denizens famously obdurate and unaffected, recessive even. Undemonstrative, straightforward and self contained, Balmamion is a stereotypical *Magninot* (colloquial Piedmontese meaning, literally, 'boilermaker') of the area: he is of Piedmont, but categorically not of Turin. In May 1962 – and still in fact today – he had no interest in the lifestyle and perceived glamour afforded to wealthy, successful sportsmen. Giacotto had given him a job to do, and he wanted no more than to accomplish it to the best of his abilities. His sole motivation was to survive at Carpano and to do that he needed to perform at the Giro.

By contrast Nino Defilippis remains, even at 74, every inch the streetwise Torinese city slicker; sharp, purposeful, expressive. He still works prodigious hours and is very much the man in charge, a born leader who likes to lead. At work Nino is completely unambiguous, he *marshals* his people. During an outstandingly successful early career he seemed destined for greatness, a natural. With his boxer's nose and furtive good looks Nino was 'The Kid', driven by a massive desire to succeed, bound for the very top. Though ultimately he never scaled the heights in the complex, often opaque business of stage-racing, Nino was capable of extraordinary single-day performances when suitably inspired, the sheer coruscating force of his ambition consuming anything, or body, that dared stand in his way. On his day he was a cycling tour de force, and a sponsor's dream. He embraced his celebrity, enthusiastically mixing with the emergent pop stars and the footballers of both 'Juve' and 'Toro', the showbiz crowd. Nino was Giacotto's captain on the road, deciding tactics, advising starry-eyed recruits, teaching the next generation the Carpano way. For this he was roundly admired, and handsomely paid. Nino's power base at Carpano was considerable, and he had no intention of seeing it diminished.

Balmamion's collapse on stage two had predicated a change in team policy, impelling Defilippis to forgo what, for a rider of his ability, was the easy glory of stage-wins in favour of the less glamorous, more prosaic business of slugging it out at the front of the race, all the time marking and being marked by Massignan, Pérez-Francés, Taccone and Battistini. He felt badly let down by the youngster, and began to harbour a sense of injustice that he, senior to and better than Franco, had been obliged to clean up after him. Whilst Defilippis, denied the chance to show his hand by team orders, tiptoed his way through the Giro, the increasingly popular young Canavese was afforded the license to express himself, for want of anything much better to do. To ride, in fact, as Nino would have chosen to do. As Balmamion's renewed form animated the race, so Defilippis' feelings of envy and abandonment grew. Nino felt that he was riding with his hands tied, picking up the bill for Franco's failure at Sestri Levante. Balmamion, having inexpertly compromised Nino's Giro, was now liberated from responsibility, able simply to enjoy the ride.

In addition Nino, a social animal, was, perhaps understandably, exasperated by Balmamion's silence which, in the circumstances, was easily mistaken for a lack of contrition. 'We shared a room but we didn't talk at all. Just an endless silence, his head turned one way, mine the other.' Though the case is unproven, it seems quite conceivable that Defilippis' abandonment of the *maglia tricolore* was not after all the act of a man seeking anonymity, but one seeking attention. Either way, for Nino, an even more harrowing sequence of events lay in wait...

Nino on the podium at Piedmont after winning the
National Championship, with Franco

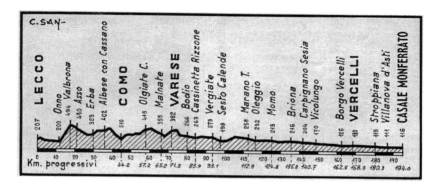

With three Alpine stages and the traditional final day promenade into Milan to follow, stage 17, a classic 232-kilometre transitional run to the vineyards of Casale Monferrato, south east of Turin, represented, in theory at least, the final opportunity for the remaining *gregari*, the unsung heroes of the Giro, to claim a breakaway stage-win. These stages traditionally offer a respite from the war of attrition that grand tour aspirants undertake, the calm before the storm as they gather themselves for the decisive mountain showdown to follow.

Immediately the riders took their leave of the starting village and rolled around Lake Lecco, Defilippis launched a ferocious 'surprise' attack, as a dangerous group of six, including Carpano's Sartore, forced Legnano onto the defensive earlier than they could have envisaged. They chased hard and, with Massignan in particular contributing heavily to the work, caught Nino's group on the climb of Onno, some 11 kilometres into the stage. *Gruppo compatto.* As the two groups conjoined, seven riders, including Carpano's Bailetti and, bizarrely, the Legnano *gregario* Manzoni, jumped out from the peloton, hopeful that theirs would be the break that stayed away. Balmamion, seeing Battistini suffering badly towards the back and sensing that Legnano were in momentary disarray following the chase, tried his luck, dragging along the Trojan Angelo Conterno and three others for good measure. To compound Battistini's distress, Massignan, apparently fearful of being seen to attack his leader, chose not to throw his lot in with the escapees but to wait. By the time

Legnano had organised themselves, the horses, all twelve of them, had bolted and the stable door was all but locked.

In checking the composition of the break Balmamion couldn't believe his good fortune. In addition to two strong *gregari,* he was joined by three hungry riders from the Molteni team – the outstanding Giro debutant Guido De Rosso, the tough veteran Fallarini and, crucially, Armando Pellegrini, from the cycling stronghold of Bergamo. Molteni, bereft of a decent GC rider, were in dire need of a stage-win, having failed miserably to land one as Faema tied the peloton in knots over the first ten days of the race. Here Pellegrini, a more than useful finisher, was the ace in the pack. Both Molteni and Carpano recognised that if the break stayed clear he would, in all probability, win the group sprint, which the Carpano trio immediately agreed not to contest. Moreover, Angelino Soler, with whom Balmamion was on good terms following the climb to Piani Resinelli, agreed to contribute (though later his peddle broke), whilst one each from San Pellegrino, Torpado and Liberia hitched a ride, hoping to break away from the breakaway as it neared the finish. All of which left the hapless Manzoni and Fabbbri, a *gregario* from Baldini's Moschettieri, praying that the cavalry, currently receding from view in the far distance, would quickly saddle up and begin the pursuit.

Now Massignan, Battistini and their faithful *gregario* Renzo Accordi, realizing the inherent danger of a Carpano/Molteni alliance, struggled frantically to organize a coalition of teams to assist in the putative chase, to no avail. In cycling, money above all else buys influence and Legnano, for all Masignan's brilliance and Pavesi's experience, didn't have any, their small budget spent on retaining the services of not one but two potential Giro winners. Consequently they found only tiredness, apathy and obstruction. Amidst the lethargy, Nino Defilippis, outraged, called the team car, insisting that Giacotto order the Carpano three back to the peloton. In what would become the defining moment of the Giro Giacotto refused, reasoning that a successful Balmamion break, and thus a further erosion of Battistini's lead, represented a win-win scenario for the team, a chance to put a second Carpano rider into a race threatening position. Incandescent, Defilippis promptly climbed off his bike. Persuaded finally to remount, he then sought to galvanise a chase, directly contrary to team orders, but without success. Crucially, hurtfully for Nino, the two remaining Carpano *gregari*, Sartore and Germano Barale, forced in effect to choose between Balmamion and

Defilippis, chose the former and refused to work. Here Carpano's lingering pretence of team unity finally unravelled as the gloves came categorically, irrevocably, off.

The escapees quickly had themselves organised, their lead increasing inexorably with each passing kilometre as they drove on at over 50kph. "We could see immediately that it was a good escape. We agreed with the Molteni three that Pellegrini would save himself for the sprint and not collaborate directly, but that the five of us would work to stay away. All five of us were really motivated and very strong that day, there was no let up. Even Soler got stuck in before his 'mechanical'. It was a fantastic ride, the kind you dream about as a cyclist."

By the time Pellegrini sprinted to claim a textbook stage-win, they had an improbable 6'44" over the peloton. More improbable still, the young eagle of Canavese, 22-year-old Franco Balmamion, he of the stage two horror show, had brilliantly crafted, and grafted for himself a *maglia rosa*, 2'21" in advance of the beleaguered Battistini.

Balmamion driving the race-winning break on stage 17

At first glance it seems impossible to comprehend the magnitude of Legnano's misjudgement. The stage was basically flat, the peloton small, attacks inevitable. Battistini and Massignan, both hardened, experienced stage racers, backed by the strongest (numerically at least) team in the Giro, simply had to ensure that the *right* break, containing only non-GC riders, stuck. What on earth went wrong?

I asked Imerio Massignan how they'd contrived to lose the pink jersey:

'First you need to understand that we weren't a team as such. We had me and Battistini and then seven others. With the exception of Accordi, all of them were young, badly paid and pretty hopeless. By and large they were out of control, did as they pleased. I saw them in the morning at breakfast, then again in the evening at dinner. They were only earning 50,000 lire because Legnano was a poor bike manufacturer and all of the budget was spent on me and Battistini, the two leaders. That was Pavesi's big mistake. If he had kept one leader instead of two, we could have had better *gregari* and a more cohesive team. Pavesi, unlike Giacotto, had no strategy, no tactical plan. He was 79 years old and, to be honest, he spent most of his time asleep in the team car. When Nino escaped I was the only one doing the pulling on the climb. Battistini had gone too deep in the Dolomites and couldn't react. By the time we caught the Defilippis group I was shattered. It's not true to say that I didn't immediately respond when Franco went. The fact is that I *couldn't* respond. I was exhausted.'

After the Giro Pavesi suggested that his leaders had wanted to conserve energy, assuming that Balmamion could easily be overhauled in the Alps.

'It's nonsense, not true at all. Pavesi said that to ease his own conscience because he was clueless. We knew Balmamion was a threat, and I knew Battistini was weakening. I nearly killed myself trying to bring that break back, as did Battistini and our only real team-mate, Accordi. We chased them for 70 kilometres, but we got no help. We were only three, and they seven, if you include Soler. They would be travelling at 60kph. I asked Baldini and Taccone to help, but they wouldn't pull at all, they gave nothing. So to say we didn't work is wrong. I was ruined when I arrived that afternoon, completely destroyed.'

Interviewed by *La Gazzetta* later after the stage, Defilippis was incoherent with rage. He ranted:

'It was made clear before the stage that they could join escapes, but not pull on the front. What happened? They worked, at my expense. What type of person would do that? This was a stage I could easily have won. I can't be philosophical about these things, I feel terribly bitter! I swear that if it were not for my faithfulness to Carpano, I would have exploded with all I have endured over the last three days. I am 30 years old. I believed I had the experience and know-how to lead this team. Evidently I was naïve!'

An angry Balmamion, unrepentant and justifiably hurt by this latest assault, finally broke his silence:

'Why should I feel guilty? The opportunity presented itself and demanded that I work. Was I to ignore it? What would have been achieved? What would the Directors of Carpano have said?'

Following this latest outburst Nino packed his bags, fled the team hotel and, after a late dinner with his fiancée and would-be parents-in-law, jumped into his car and proceeded to drive the 75 kilometres to Turin, his Giro apparently over. However, as he pulled up outside his house at 3a.m., he found waiting on his driveway Giacotto, Carpano's owner, Attilio Turati, and his own good friend Bertazzini, the cycling photographer of *Tutto Sport*. There followed a lengthy 'discussion' before Turati, fearful of the PR disaster unfolding before him, wrote Nino a cheque for one million lire – nearly three months salary for Franco Balmamion – whereupon the Torinese hopped (and presumably skipped and jumped) back into his car and drove back to the hotel, his appetite for the Giro miraculously restored.

Nino's two hours of sleep were thus spent in an otherwise empty hotel room that early morning. By way of calming the nerves of his stressed out *maglia rosa* Giacotto had invited cool, amicable Toni Bailetti to share with Franco. Game on.

THE SPIDER OF THE DOLOMITES

Following Gaul's exhilarating last gasp capture of the 1959 Giro, that year's Tour de France, the most eagerly awaited for a decade, descended into a parochial, internecine squabble. Rival French teams, headed respectively by Anglade and Anquetil, sought not so much to win as, overwhelmingly, to see one another lose. The upshot was a wasted race, mired in uncertainty, a sterile tactical gluepot. Chief benefactor was the Spanish climbing ace Bahamontes, a brilliant, although some said slightly fortuitous winner. France, expecting better from her sporting heroes, was officially disgusted.

For its 1960 edition the Giro, perpetually playing a (losing) game of catch-up with its wealthier, more prestigious cousin, wanted at all costs for Anquetil, the new superstar of world cycling, to further bolster its reputation by again challenging Nencini and Gaul. By way of encouragement they included three juicy time trials and Anquetil, anxious to avenge his humiliating defeat of the previous year, was easily seduced, all too ready to put the Luxemburger (one of the few in the peloton for whom he had little time) firmly in his place.

Two weeks into the race, Imerio '*Gamba Secca*' Massignan, in the best climbing form of his life, lay second overall, 1'27" behind the surprise leader, Hoevenaers. The fourteenth stage, a hilly 68-kilometre time trial, found his Giro aspirations, and those of virtually all of the home based riders, reduced to dust as he conceded over nine minutes to a magnificent Anquetil. Though apparently disastrous in the context of the race, Massignan's performance wasn't quite as shabby as would first appear. Anquetil had devoured the course at such a rate that 70 riders found themselves outside the time limit, compelling the organizers to rewrite a rule book specifying that anybody finishing over 12% in arrears would automatically be removed from the race.

By the penultimate stage, a 230-kilometre Dolomite odyssey, Massignan, rubber-stamping his excellence in the mountains, had rallied to a commendable sixth position, seven minutes in arrears to the Frenchman. Anquetil led second-placed Nencini by three minutes with Gaul, too, out of contention at over seven minutes. The stage saw the introduction of a new climb, the 2,600-metre Passo Di Gavia, hailed by Luigi Chierici, cycling correspondent of the sports weekly *Stadio*, as 'potentially the greatest of all cycling's theatres, much longer and steeper than the Izoard of Coppi, Bartali and poor Robic, much harder than the Iseran'. Pictures of the day reveal that the climb, described by race director Vincenzo Torriani as his 'beautiful monster', was in large part little more than a mud heap: unpaved, strewn with rocks and very occasionally dangerous, broken asphalt. And at 17 kilometres murderously, hatefully long.

Rik Van Looy, out of overall contention but keen to demonstrate his credentials as a climber, and to claim the cash on offer for the victor of the King of the Mountains competition, took off early in the company of, amongst others, his dutiful lieutenant, Edgard Sorgeloos. As his fellow escapees fell away, Van Looy claimed the points over the first two climbs before, close to the summit of the penultimate mountain, Passo Tonale, he found himself joined by a rampant Imerio Massignan. The two quickly found the mutual stimulus of agreement. Van Looy had eaten all of his food and was by now becoming hungry, while Massignan had two precious, priceless panini. For his part Imerio, keen to improve his overall position, reasoned that a refuelled Van Looy, a tremendous bike handler, may have his uses on the downhill, in the valley and, assuming there remained something in his tank, conceivably on the ascent of the Gavia. He not only gave Van Looy his last panino, but allowed the Belgian maximum points over the top. With Massignan every bit Van Looy's equal, the two barrelled down the Tonale and through the valley. They hit the final mountain together in incessant, freezing rain before, barely onto the lower slopes, Van Looy capitulated so completely that by the finish he would lose in excess of 40 minutes. A supercharged Massignan, turning a massive gear through the mud and sloshing snow, over and around the stones, hammered on alone, all the while inflicting greater damage on Gaul, Nencini and the panic stricken, incredulous Anquetil. By the time he crested the pass he'd put almost two minutes into Gaul, an astonishing five into Nencini and the panicking *maglia rosa*. From nowhere Massignan, a much more competent descender than the increasingly ragged Anquetil, had the queen stage of the race in his pocket and had a shot, a pretty decent one at that, at winning the Giro.

What followed remains one of the more absurd episodes in the history of a race given at the best of times to eccentricity. First the Legnano team car blew its head gasket, leaving Massignan bereft not only of food but also support, moral and mechanical. Unperturbed, *Gamba Secca*, on the ride of his life, continued to hurl his bike brilliantly down the mountain. Seven kilometres into the descent the unthinkable – a back tyre puncture. In a scene reminiscent of the great pre-war era, Massignan pulled a spare from his jersey, pumped it up as best his frozen hands would allow, got back on the bike and continued his plunge towards Bormio, the stage finish. Implausibly, five minutes later he punctured *again*, the same wheel, and, as a disbelieving Charly Gaul charged past, was forced to commandeer a wheel from a spectating amateur rider. Driven now to a furious, maniacal time trialing descent, Imerio Massignan again overhauled the flagging Gaul three kilometres from the finish. Finally, nearing the stage finish, contemplating the fates which had cruelly deprived him of an historic Giro win but which had afforded him by way of consolation the most epic of stages and a podium finish overall, Massignan suffered the desperate, despicable ignominy of a third puncture, this time to the front tyre. Only this time of course, he was all out of spares, obliged to ride home as best he could on the rim. Twenty metres – *twenty metres* – from the finishing line, big-hearted Gaul added to his growing canon of 'epic' stage-wins by sneaking sheepishly by the stricken Massignan to claim the stage victory. Another great Charly Gaul exploit.

Anquetil clung on to win the Giro by the narrowest of margins from Nencini, with Gaul third and Massignan, utterly inconsolable, in fourth place. Had he chosen, been more calculating, Massignan could easily have deprived Rik Van Looy of the King of the Mountains competition. Instead, sensing that the Flemish was beginning to struggle, he gave him the remainder of his lunch and allowed him maximum points. Had the ailing, neglected Legnano team car not blown up he would certainly have won the stage, absolutely have finished at least second in the Giro. Had he not punctured at all he would probably have won the 1960 Giro d'Italia, though when I interviewed him at home 47 years later, he was much too modest to admit it, conceding, when pushed, only that, while Nencini and Anquetil were *Signori,* Gaul had behaved like a *bastardino*.

The upside to all this? At least they stopped calling him *Gamba Secca*. The legend of the 'Spider of the Dolomites' – *Ragno delle Dolomiti* – surely the greatest, most evocative of all the cycling nicknames, was born.

Imerio Massignan, the 'Spider of the Dolomites'

Imerio Massignan very nearly didn't become a cyclist at all. Though all but unbeatable uphill (he won 20 races in his last year as an amateur), by aged 21 he was working full time as a mechanic at a FIAT dealership, waiting for a call that never seemed to come. By the time Pavesi picked up the phone in April 1959, Imerio, thought by some to lack the killer instinct needed amongst the professionals to complement his outstanding physical gifts, was beginning to lose faith. Of the dozen or so former cyclists I interviewed in researching this book, Massignan was, by some considerable distance, the most open and honest, the most charming and self-effacing. These same qualities, whilst endearing him greatly to the public and to his team-mates, were often to prove his undoing in the unscrupulous, winner-take-all world of the peloton. As he recounts his stories of cruel misfortune (and there is such a litany of near misses and hard luck stories that even he struggles to believe how one rider could be blighted by such bad luck so often) Imerio does so with an occasional rueful smile, though never once does he betray the merest hint of resentment. He knows full well that Vito Taccone cheated him out of the Tour of Lombardy, and out of a considerable sum of money offered but never paid for his help at Tirreno–Adriatico, Italy's second most prestigious stage-race. He understands perfectly that Gaul stiffed him at the Giri of 1959 and 1960. Massignan knows that his loyalty to Legnano was misplaced when the bigger, higher paying teams came knocking in 1960 and that, had he been better supported, had the cards fallen his way, he and not Balmamion could quite easily have won the 1962 Giro d'Italia. He knows that the kidney infection he suffered in training for the 1963 season effectively finished him as a grand tour protagonist, though he carried on failing to win bike races until 1970.

At first glance Imerio Massignan's *palmarés* makes for pretty average reading for a rider of his exceptional gifts: a solitary stage-win at the Tour; some near misses at the Giro and the Tour of Romandie; a couple of King of the Mountains jerseys in France; the odd stage victory in the Tour of Catalonia. And yet, here today with him in his modest Piedmontese house, the occasional winning and endless losing doesn't seem to matter at all. It matters not to me and certainly not to Mario, who's simply in awe of the man, as were a generation of Italian cycling fans almost fifty years ago. What matters with Imerio Massignan, the best climber you've probably never heard of, is the man himself, his exhilarating power in the mountains, his humility and generosity in life. Imerio Massignan's greatness (and make no mistake that greatness it is – he was recently voted into Italian cycling's Hall of Fame ahead of the twice World Champion and Giro winner, Gianni Bugno) lies not in the winning but in the refusing to be beaten. Because that, as any half-decent cyclist will tell you, is precisely the point. That's precisely what cycling is.

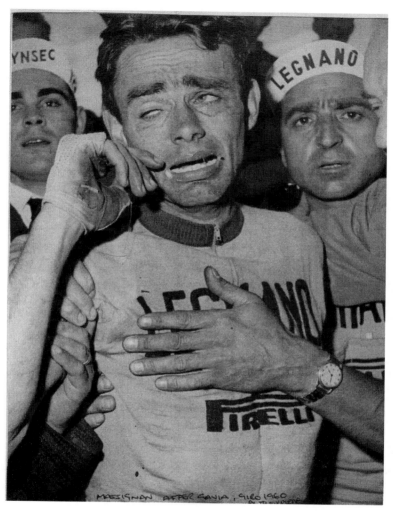

Massignan after the finish of the Garvia stage, Giro 1960

STAGE EIGHTEEN

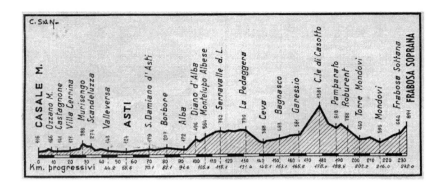

Stage eighteen saw a wrung-out, depleted peloton reach the Piedmontese Maritime Alps, though not before a leaden, 165-kilometre, five-hour sightseeing procession through Monferrato and the Langhe, the rolling, verdant wine producing areas similar in topography to picture postcard Tuscany. Due south the pack dawdled through the great thirteenth century fortress cities of Asti and Alba to bland, matter-of-fact Ceva, another of those featureless Piedmontese towns the local tourist office struggles to make a case for. Let's just say that Ceva, unlike poor Villadossola, has an excellent ring road.

By the time the racing began in earnest at Garessio, 70 kilometres from home and starting point of a 12-kilometre mountain pass, the testing Colle di Cassotto, the peloton was already an hour behind schedule. When Defilippis punctured on the climb, Taccone attacked, leaving Balmamion exposed as the Carpano *gregari* buckled. The *maglia rosa* held ground until Taccone went again on the descent, a dangerous beaten earth plunge, and here the elastic snapped as the Abruzzese, Pérez-Francés, Massignan and the fast improving Adorni escaped with Guido Neri. By the time the race reached Mondovì, 16 kilometres of solid uphill from the finish, the five had 30 seconds on a group of 11, containing, amongst others, Balmamion, Battistini, Soler and Desmet. Decision time for the *maglia rosa* – big, crucial, ugly stick-or-twist decision time.

Sixteen kilometres is a hell of a long way to lead a pursuit uphill, particularly if you've done two massive rides the days before, as Franco Balmamion had. There was no way that Battistini would take the initiative, given that his team-mate Massignan stood to gain vital time, while the others, Desmet included, would be foolhardy to lead the chase with the *maglia rosa* in their midst. Balmamion had everything to lose; he alone was responsible for catching the lead group. Strangely though, the race leader didn't attempt to lead the charge across to the Taccone group. Strangely instead, he waited ... and waited.

Franco Balmamion realised that in staying with the group he would be in the company of the Ghigi pair of Antonio Suarez and Angelino Soler. Soler, out of overall contention and thus under no pressure to work hard every day, had chosen his stages carefully and, in so doing, preserved his strength to prove himself the most devastating climber in the Giro, a serial stage-winner and King of the Mountains. Balmamion was shrewd enough to realise that Soler, a racing certainty to win the stage from the position they found themselves in, was the best wheel to follow towards the inordinately steep final four kilometres. No way would his team-mate Suarez, an outstanding climber in his own right, allow the gap to grow with another stage-win, more King of the Mountains points and another bag of cash up for easy grabs. Sure enough, the two Spaniards rode the *maglia rosa* back into contention before Suarez peeled off exhausted, leaving Soler to systematically dismantle the lead group as the gradients became sheer. By the time the Spaniard reached the finishing line in little under seven and a half hours, Balmamion had ceded just 23 seconds to Battistini and Pérez-Francés, 15 to Taccone and nothing at all to the ailing Massignan. Defilippis, towed grudgingly along the valley by Sartore and Barale ('I was tempted to leave him there'), surrendered just 21 seconds, a remarkable achievement in the light of his bludgeoned moral and lack of sleep.

Asked where he'd found the strength to endure, Balmamion replied:

'I knew I would suffer today but I only had one main concern, I was worried about puncturing. Those people amazed that I didn't capitulate obviously don't realise that I've always been at my best in the mountains. All things considered my first day in the *maglia rosa* wasn't too bad. Although I lost a little time I felt I climbed as well as anybody, with the possible exception of Battistini.'

With the combined might of the five chastened favourites unleashed against him, this was an heroic performance by the young race leader, as intelligent and tenacious as the ride to Casale had been opportunistic. Over the bruising final 70 kilometres Balmamion had survived, manfully if not entirely comfortably, against the very best the Giro could offer. What's more he'd been strong enough to catch Massignan on the final climb, while Taccone's big attack had been fruitless, leaving him, along with Nino, over five minutes in arrears and all but out of contention. With just two competitive stages remaining, Balmamion led Battistini by 1'58" with Pérez-Francés third at 2'29" and the brilliant Massignan fourth at 3'39".

Franco supported by team-manager Vincenzo Giacotto

STAGE NINETEEN

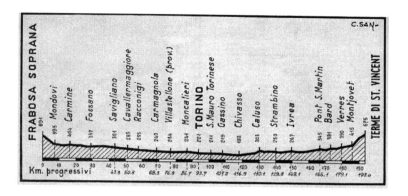

The *maglia rosa* hung in again, though not without alarm, on stage 19. The day comprised a due north hike directly through the heart of downtown Turin to the ski resort town of Saint Vincent. Though shortish at 193 kilometres, the stage was dead flat (and as such well outside of Balmamion's comfort zone) save for a seven-kilometre kick-up to the finish. Early on in proceedings Carpano's Giuseppe Sartore slipped clear of the pack in the company of a Giro rookie, 21-year-old Aldo Beraldo of Torpado. As the race hit his home city, Defilippis blatantly lit the blue touch paper, attacking Balmamion and inciting a group of eight others, including Battistini, Massignan and Pérez-Francés, to join him. A bewildered Toni Bailetti accidently found himself in the lead group:

> 'It was a ferocious break, absolutely ferocious. I was all over the place, wanting to help Franco, not wishing to upset Nino, whilst trying desperately not to do any work. I wanted to tell Nino to ride for the team and not for himself, but it was impossible to speak to him, he was really wild. I couldn't do right for doing wrong.'

The race leader was thus compelled to form an impromptu, cap-in-hand alliance with two rival teams (Philco and Moschettieri) in organising to chase down his own team-mate, *his own erstwhile room-mate*. They finally reeled them in at Cimena, some 20 frantic kilometres up the road, before Sartore saw off Beraldo to claim the first and best win of what would prove a decent career spent by and large helping Franco Balmamion.

Despite Nino's sleight of hand, Balmamion declared himself pleased with the stage and with his form going into the decisive stage of the Giro:

'I feel quite confident. I enjoy riding in the Alps and I know the area well. I won my first ever race there back in 1959, and I have ridden well there since. I just hope that the area is as kind to me again on this, the most important day of my life.'

Meanwhile, unbeknown to Franco, Uncle Ettore, persuaded to make a rare excursion to Turin to support his boy, was robbed of his wallet and the 60,000 lire it contained, which rather put the dampers on the Balmamion clan's big day out in the city. No matter, their boy wonder was the man in possession of the two-and-a-half-million lire *maglia rosa*. Could he hold on for the paydirt?

With one competitive stage remaining Balmamion had, amidst a near epidemic of incredulity, all but won the Giro d'Italia. Only 48 warriors remained as the race glimpsed the promised land, Milan's famous Vigorelli velodrome.

Balmamion, Defilippis amd Angelo Conterno, the 'White Feather'

STAGE TWENTY

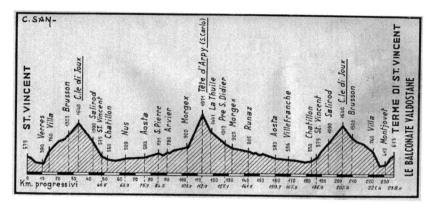

At 5.30 on the morning of Friday 8th June, Nino Defilippis and Franco Balmamion were woken for the obligatory cyclist's breakfast of boiled rice and steak, and for an earlier than was decent appointment with the penultimate, decisive day of the Giro. The stage, rolling out of St. Vincent at 8.40, would see the race reach its northernmost point – two ascents of the notorious Col di Joux sandwiching the hateful Colle San Carlo, a hitherto unclimbed, unpaved ten-kilometre brute, with a punishing average gradient of over 11%. Uncharted territory for the race, an undreamt of opportunity for Franco Balmamion, a final, desperate shake of the dice for the favourites. At the Carpano team meeting Milano and Giacotto outlined the strategy for the day, such as it was. Conterno, Barale and Bailetti were to stay close to Balmamion for as long as possible, then to ensure Carpano retained enough *gregari* for a strong showing in Milan, while Sartore was required simply to survive inside the time limit, following his heroic but debilitating exploit of the previous day. For his part Defilippis was charged with protecting the *maglia rosa* throughout, to keep the lid on the Legnano pair and on Pérez-Francés, to chase down the dangerous Taccone's inevitable attacks, be ready to offer a wheel should Balmamion puncture. In short, to redeem himself by riding as a loyal team-mate ought.

Giacotto's appeal for solidarity predictably fell on deaf ears. Scandalously, on the first ascent of the Joux a mutinous Defilippis attacked, determined to rain on Balmamion's victory parade. Nino's act of insolence succeeded only in shelling out both Pérez-Francés and Battistini, the very riders he sought to promote, from the lead group. Poetic justice? Quite possibly, though Balmamion, a young man not given to dealing in such abstracts, once more applied the most valuable commodity in the professional cyclists' armoury, that of common sense under intense physical and mental strain. Buoyed by Battistini's evident fatigue and by his own continued good form, he cannily glued himself to Nino's back wheel as Angelino Soler jumped away to claim the mountains points at the summit. In the valley bottom an escape group of three, led by Nino Assirelli, anxious to restore some credibility to the Moschettieri, sneaked clear of the re-forming peloton. Here, mindful of the severity of the climb to follow, Balmamion replaced his back wheel, fitting a bigger block in anticipation of the impending deluge of attacks. Balmamion generally employed a gear ratio of 42x21 (much bigger than today's riders typically use), but calculated this would not be low enough for the extreme gradients of the San Carlo, where he fully expected the blitz to begin in earnest. There he would need 42x25.

At Morgex, on the lower slopes, the peloton began to fracture as Massignan, Adorni and Defilippis joined forces to begin the merciless culling of the weak, the lame and the irresolute. Amongst the early casualties were Battistini and Pérez-Francés, spectacularly and this time irreversibly dropped. Both would concede six minutes, their Giro pretensions cruelly and definitively exposed. By the summit, with Defilippis unable to impose his considerable will on proceedings, and with Battistini out of the reckoning, Balmamion's lead had increased to a *de facto* three and a half minutes over Imerio Massignan. Moreover, he'd responded easily to the onslaught and felt confident that neither Taccone nor Defilippis could hurt him on the final climb of the Giro. Only the great climber Massignan had the ammunition for that, and his form looked pretty shakey. Nearly there, then, but not quite.

A further re-grouping on the descent saw 13 riders reach the bottom together, with the *maglia rosa*, as consummate downhill as up, apparently comfortable towards the front of the bunch. Worryingly though, with the exception of Nino, nobody remained from Carpano. Now alone and exposed, Balmamion was presented with a single final obstacle – the valley:

'I had a big problem. They knew I had to change my wheel again ready for the last climb. I'd pleaded with Nino to ride tempo but he wasn't interested. He wanted to catch Assirelli, to get a stage-win. I had the feeling that if in the process I lost the jersey then so much the better. It was 50 kilometres to the Joux and I knew he, Taccone and Massignan would attack me. If I lost contact I could still lose the Giro. I was worried.'

How best to deal with the enemy within?

'First I decided I'd wait until we hit the climb before changing the wheel. That way the time I lost could be recovered easily. I was still climbing very strongly. My only concern beyond that was that I might puncture in the valley, in which case Taccone, Nino and Massignan would collaborate and drop me. In the group were two riders from Torpado, Guido Neri and Nunzio Pellicciari. Torpado was a small team and I knew their riders were quite poorly paid. They'd hardly earned anything at the Giro, and there was no way either of them could win the stage. I got on well with Neri and asked them if they were interested in earning some cash. We settled on 300,000 lire and they protected me in the valley. Neri in particular was really strong. Good money for them for an hour or so of work.'

Safely on to the Joux Balmamion re-installed his 42x21 back wheel, recovered the 20 or so seconds lost in so doing, then simply bided his time, confident that Taccone, though all but spent, was capable of responding to Defilippis' increasingly desperate surges. Following the collapse of Battistini and Pérez-Francés, Defilippis and Taccone were effectively racing for a podium finish, so Balmamion's logic was, as ever, flawless. In allowing Taccone to react to Nino's violent accelerations he was able to ride well within himself. Towards the summit Defilippis, seeking the King of the Mountains points and finally to reel in Assirelli, launched a last stinging attack, at which point the exhausted Imerio Massignan cracked. Here Balmamion, his extraordinary Giro d'Italia secured, graciously allowed Defilippis, though not Taccone, to ride away.

On the final descent into St Vincent Nino punctured, heaping insult upon injury. As Balmamion and Taccone flew by, a stricken, deluded Defilippis once more saw red, blurting out a stream of obscenities. For his part, Balmamion first slowed, then towed Defilippis to the finish line as Taccone, second on the stage behind Assirelli, failed by 19 seconds to overhaul Nino. With Massignan rallying somewhat to claim second place, Defilippis thus secured third place overall. It was a measure of his decency that the Canavese chose to help not humiliate him.

More polemics followed during the post-stage media scrum. Churlish to the last, Nino claimed that Balmamion and Taccone had reached an 'accord', inferring that the *maglia rosa* had paid the Abruzzese to neutralize his attacks. Though the trading of favours is as old as the sport itself, Nino's suggestion that Franco had bought the southern reprobate Taccone constituted a further thinly veiled assault on Balmamion's character and abilities. Taccone was a southern outcast gobshite; no *real* holder of the pink jeresey would fraternize with his like.

Oddly enough, Imerio Massignan told me during our interview that Nino had approached him to work together to break Balmamion on the San Carlo, but that the race leader was 'incredibly strong'.

Characteristically Balmamion played the diplomat. Asked whether Nino had helped on the stage he replied:

'We are in full accord. The result today was favourable for me. Nino at least deserved the satisfaction of a stage-win. I am sorry that he didn't quite manage it.'

Would it have been easier to defend the jersey without Defilippis in the team?

'Who can say? Perhaps yes, perhaps no. Surely, though, it's better that Nino is here?'

Later that evening Balmamion received a visit from Guido Neri, paid the 300,000 lire cash (borrowed from Giacotto), then went quietly to his bed, dreaming dreams of Milan and of the sanctuary of home, his incredible mission accomplished.

And had he? Paid Taccone?

'Paid Taccone? Are you serious? *Vito Taccone?* Never!'

Nino thus concluded the Giro much as he'd begun it. Barking up the wrong tree.

HUMAN RESOURCES

Franco Balmamion, though by his own admission not yet the greatest of riders, was already at 22 proving himself amongst the cutest and most pragmatic of his generation. In utilizing Neri and Pellicciari Balmamion had been acutely aware that in the peloton at least, it paid to have allies, as many as possible, in the right places.

Cycling history is awash with talented riders who, for whatever reason, failed to heed this most rudimentary of lessons, invariably to the detriment of their careers. Most notable was the Limousin Raymond Poulidor. Poulidor, representative of *la France profonde,* the utopian, largely imagined 'deep' France of Catholic probity and a profound attachment to the *le pays*, was lionised by the French public, who adored his dull, country-boy good looks, simple racing style and perceived lack of sophistication. Poulidor thought himself 'of the people', whilst his *bête noir,* Anquetil, a blonde haired, blue eyed Normand, was largely despised for his supposed coldness (he was in fact chronically shy and insecure, all at sea with the media), his Anglo-Saxon appearance and for an extra-marital affair which scandalised all of France, paralleling Coppi's experience in Italy a decade previously. Though by no means a paragon of virtue, Anquetil understood intuitively the fellowship, forged in the long hours of communal suffering, which lies at the heart of Professional cycling, the glue that binds the peloton. Vin Denson spent three outstanding years in Anquetil's service, between 1965 and 1967. Vin is unequivocal:

'I loved Jacques. I would have died on the road for him. We all would. He could suffer on a bike more than anyone else I ever saw, but above all he was an absolute gentleman. I'd spent the previous year working for Rik Van Looy, flogging my guts out, never being paid what I was due, always feeling cheated. The years I spent with Jacques were the happiest of my life, without question. The whole peloton respected him. Poulidor liked to be centre of attention, but within the peloton we knew him for what he was – a fabulous rider, but by comparison a bit selfish, nowhere near Jacques' class.'

Anquetil's many detractors abhored what they took to be his calculating racing style: untouchable against the stopwatch, entirely reactive and expedient in the mountains – a blueprint for grand tour success. On the road though, where it really mattered, Anquetil was a tremendously popular figure, universally respected and admired. Anquetil made it his business to be one of the proletariat, to be on good terms with even the most junior riders. In so doing he ensured that his team of distinguished shop stewards, hard men like Stablinski, Novak and the brilliant Irishman, Shay Elliott, had the ear of the peloton. They were by and large able to dictate the pattern and shape of races, trading favours with rival teams, throwing bones if necessary to the needy, co-opting willing *domestiques* from outside as the need arose. So great was their leader's influence and standing, that on occasion it must have seemed to Poulidor that the entire peloton was riding in support of his tormentor. Little wonder that in the two-horse race which was the Tour de France in the early 1960s, 'Pou-Pou' was 'the eternal second'.

The flipside, of course, was that both Anquetil and Coppi were condemned in the court of public opinion. For winning too easily for too long, Coppi in particular was vilified beyond reasonable measure. A goodly, simple man with a prodigious talent for riding a bicycle quickly, Coppi found himself exiled in his own country as the Italian media, by turns sanctimonious *and* salacious, put the boot in, a genuine human tragedy.

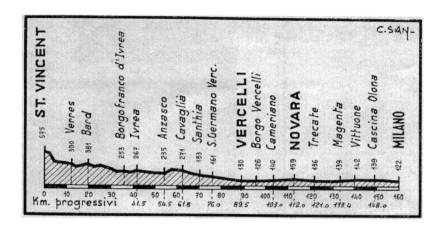

The Giro's final stage, the traditional 160-kilometre procession to Milan's Vigorelli velodrome, passed off without major incident, though Franco Balmamion felt some discomfort in his right knee, he believes probably a result of a crash he'd suffered at the previous year's race. Defilippis, in principle the best sprinter remaining in the peloton and thus theoretically a good bet here, failed depressingly to secure his stage-win, beaten conclusively and harrowingly into seventh as Guido Carlesi once more showed his class, comfortably winning one of the slowest stages in post-war Giro history.

Afterwards, while Nino blustered obtusely about 'the self-justification of the winner', Franco confirmed that he had no interest in riding the Tour de France and steadfastly, quite correctly in the circumstances, refuted all suggestion of a falling-out. Throughout the Giro, and in spite of all Nino's provocation, Balmamion never once retaliated, directly or otherwise:

'I never had a problem with Nino as such. We fell out later at a criterium race but it was over nothing. I understood his frustration and I knew I was being provoked, but I chose not to confront him, and he never actually said anything to me directly. At the end I was tired; I'd had enough and wanted just to get home to celebrate with my people. I let the media draw their own conclusions.'

Luigi Gianoli – Lo Sport Illustrato 14/6/ 1962
'So the Giro is finished. A story full of light and shade and of confusion and contradiction. One is left with the overriding impression that cycling, even in a battle that can seem absurd, at times even banal, is still able to produce displays of the very best human values, values that re-affirm our lives, lift us from the conformity and confusion of our everyday existence. These are not 'cultural', but simple values found in simple souls, not those of the corporate structures that often support the great sportsmen. And for that, above all, we should be grateful … Balmamion won the Giro by winning a trial of strength with his own captain, Defilippis. He showed character unimaginable in one so young, particularly one as quiet as he.'

Bruno Raschi, Lo Sport Illustrato, 14/6/62:
'In the end it was not true that this was a Giro exclusively for Taccone, Gaul and Massignan. It was, like all the Giri which have preceded it, a race for the courageous. And yet, because the favourites displayed so little courage, they contrived to lose to a young rider prepared to take chances, to truly suffer and to make things happen. Three times during the final week Balmamion simply tried his luck. As a result, he won by a process of elimination. Those who suggest he is a lucky winner should remember that he rode supremely in support of Defilippis on the stage to Passo Rolle, then carried the fight to Pian di Resinelli and (who would have imagined it?) to Casale Monferrato.

The only significant threat to Balmamion emerged on the Frabosa stage, the protagonist a mutinous Nino Defilippis. Defilippis, resistant to any sense of responsibility, was also the last to attack the *maglia rosa* on the Valdostana stage won by Assirelli.

We therefore simply recall the facts: a deserving winner; the re-birth of Baldini; the sad demise of Gaul; the debilitating see-saw of Battistini and Massignan, unsure to the last of their respective roles; the emergence of a new generation of riders, the likes of Meco and Adorni, Neri and Beraldo.

Balmamion knew he had to rise above the contradictions. He won the Giro in spite of Defilippis in a demonstration of strength and character, belying his age and quiet exterior.'

Final general classification, 1962 Giro d'Italia:

1. Franco Balmamion	Carpano		123h 07' 03"
2. Imerio Massignan	Legnano	@	3'57"
3. Nino Defilippis	Carpano	@	5'02"
4. Vito Taccone	Atala	@	5'21"
5. Vittorio Adorni	Philco	@	7'11"
6. José Pérez-Francés	Ferrys	@	7'29"
7. Ercole Baldini	Moschettieri	@	7'54"
8. Graziano Battistini	Legnano	@	8'05"
9. Guido Carlesi	Philco	@	14'22"
10. Armand Desmet	Faema	@	15'55"
11. Antonio Suarez	Ghigi	@	19'42"
12. Angelino Soler	Ghigi	@	20'00"
13. Gastone Nencini	Moschettieri	@	24'51"
23.Germano Barale	Carpano	@	1h17'41"
24.Guido Neri	Torpado	@	1h21'22"
39.Antonio Bailetti	Carpano	@	3h03'07"
47. (last) Fedele Rubagotti	Legnano	@	4h08'47"

DNF 83 riders (including: Charly Gaul, Rik Van Looy, Walter Martin, Vincenzo Meco, Arnaldo Pambianco, Henri Anglade, Joseph Carrara, Bruno Mealli)

King of the Mountains: Angelino Soler
Team classification: Faema

A pensive Franco Balmamion, Vigorelli Velodrome, Milan

Carpano disunited: Balmamion and Defilippis after the finish

PART THREE

THE SILENT CHAMPION

A POUND OF FLESH

The opening stage of the 1963 Giro d'Italia, from Naples to Potenza, was won superbly and prodigiously by Vittorio Adorni. Adorni, strongly fancied to succeed Franco Balmamion, first powered away from the peloton, then time trialed to a famous win, almost three minutes in advance of the second-placed rider. An astonishing, breathtaking performance and a clear statement of intent from a young man apparently destined for greatness. Or perhaps not. Adorni contrived to lose the leader's jersey on stage four, missing the crucial break as the powerful former *maglia tricolore,* Diego Ronchini, assumed command.

Stage seven, a beautiful, classic 174-kilometre Tuscan up hill and down dale, saw Adorni, again in outstanding form, lead a four-man escape comprising the strong Spaniard Florit Alomar, the Giro debutant Giancarlo Ceppi and, amazingly, Nino Defilippis of Carpano. Beseeched by his director, Giacotto, to ride in support of the reigning champion where circumstances dictated, Nino shamefully chose an altogether different path. In direct, flagrant abuse of Giacotto's good faith, Nino, acutely aware of the damaging consequences to Balmamion of a further Adorni incursion, chose to drive the breakaway. Presented with an opportunity to right the wrongs of the previous year and to disrupt Adorni's advance, Nino instead chose Nino, seduced once more by the easy money of a stage-win. He'd have his pound of flesh.

The breakaway succeeded. Nino had his customary 'brilliant' win as Adorni, ecstatic at his good fortune, gratefully accepted the best part of two minutes advantage over a wounded, incredulous Franco Balmamion.

Late that evening a furious Balmamion, the champion of silence, stepped quietly from his hotel room and tapped ever–so–gently on Vincenzo Giacotto's door. Overnight Defilippis, evidently weakened by his latest feat of daring-do, found himself struck down by an 'acute bronchial infection' and abandoned the Giro.

Stage ten of the race departed La Spezia for Piedmont, culminating at Asti, Piedmont's famously wealthy truffle capital. Here Vito Taccone, already out of the reckoning on GC, but always able to punch above his weight in a sprint, led home a seven-man breakaway. Taccone triumphed again the following day as the race climbed to the 13th century Monastary at Oropa, preceding Adorni by three seconds, Balmamion by nine, and the *maglia rosa* Ronchini by the best part of two minutes. Balmamion thus climbed to second overall, 29 seconds behind Ronchini, four seconds in advance of Giorgio Zancanaro. North and across the Swiss border for stage twelve, Taccone completed an unlikely hat trick as Balmamion, neck and neck over two mountain passes with Adorni, wrestled a tenuous *maglia rosa* from Ronchini's grasp. The top five contenders (Balmamion, Zancanaro, Guido De Rosso, Ronchini and Adorni) were covered by a little over two minutes in the most exciting Giro for years.

The following day, still more sensationally, Taccone produced a carbon copy, easily defeating Zancanaro, Balmamion *et al* in another seven-man climbing showdown. Though the Abruzzese, recording a fourth consecutive stage-win, unprecedented in post-war *Giri*, understandably took the plaudits, Franco's performance that day was, in the context of the race to win the Giro, particularly noteworthy. He punctured five kilometres from the finish, whereupon Taccone and Zancanaro immediately attacked, opening a 30-second gap as the race leader waited on his team car. After the tyre change Balmamion produced the finest descent of his career, latching on to the group in the final kilometre to retain his pink jersey.

Stage sixteen saw the re-introduction of the time trial, a 56-kilometre circuit of Treviso. Here Balmamion, the consummate climber, struggled vainly against the specialists, conceding 1'24" to Ronchini, and a calamitous 3'50" to stage-winner Adorni. Ronchini again led the Giro from the resurgent Adorni, with Balmamion a faltering third.

Stage eighteen, an epic Dolomite showdown, saw Ronchini capitulate as the 1961 winner Pambianco, a shadow of the Olympic gold medalist and grand tour winner he had been, salvaged a little pride with a stage victory. Here Balmamion and Adorni, crossing the line together third and fourth respectively, each sought to land the decisive knockout blow. Thus, on the eve of the queen stage of the 1963 Giro d'Italia, an exact doppelganger of Vincenzo Meco's truncated, blizzard interrupted leg into Moena the previous year, Vittorio Adorni regained the *maglia rosa* with a 22-second advantage over the young Eagle of Canavese. Zancanaro lay third at 56 seconds with young De Rosso a further 23 seconds in arrears. Unbelievably, a mere 79 seconds separated the four rivals.

The next morning Balmamion spotted Adorni and Vito Taccone in animated conversation at the roll-out. This he thought unusual, and suspicious. Taccone, fifteen minutes in arrears, couldn't realistically win the Giro, but he was a mercenary individual who fancied himself as a wheeler-dealer. Furthermore, Adorni had no great time for him in the normal course of events and as such, as the defending champion saw it, something must have been afoot.

Taccone, left to his own devices by the favourites, attacked early in the stage, taking along a local youngster named Enzo Moser and Carpano's best remaining *gregario*, the brilliant Torinese neo pro Italo Zilioli. In view of Carpano's concern about a possible agreement between Taccone and Adorni, Giacotto had charged Zilioli with keeping watch on Taccone and, in so doing, making himself available to his leader should the need arise later in the stage. Taccone proceeded to ride away from Zilioli on the penultimate climb as the youngster took his foot off the gas, saving himself in the event that Balmamion might need his assistance on the Rolle. On and on Taccone drove and, by the time he reached the foot of the Passo Rolle, he'd increased his advantage on the group containing Adorni, Balmamion and Zancanaro to a race-threatening ten minutes. Fourth placed De Rosso, no natural climber, fell quickly out of contention. Adorni, apparently fearful that the Abruzzese might renege on their agreement and hijack the *maglia rosa*, implored Balmamion to assist in chasing him down. Balmamion thought about it momentarily, then pointedly refused to collaborate. He knew that deals with Vito Taccone had a habit of coming unstuck, but calculated that Taccone couldn't possibly keep up such a ferocious pace. Balmamion felt confident that he had the legs to attack and drop Adorni further up the climb and, anyway, the pink jersey was Adorni's to defend and so, having tried to be smart in enlisting Taccone's 'help', defend it he ought. Adorni, his bluff called, was panicked, along with Zancanaro, into a frantic pursuit while Balmamion sat in the wheels, biding his time, watching and waiting, doing his thing. Now Zancanaro blew spectacularly, paying dearly for his naïvete in charging after Taccone. And then there were two...

Half way up the Passo Rolle Franco Balmamion decided that now would be a good enough time to win the Giro d'Italia. Sensing Adorni's discomfort, he began very steadily to wind up the pace – and to wind up the challenger's already escalating stress levels. Here the *maglia rosa*, unable to shake off Franco's challenge and unsure of Taccone's intentions, became increasingly ragged. As Balmamion half-wheeled him round a tight left-handed switchback, Adorni momentarily lost concentration and balance, his peddle catching on the asphalt. It cost him ten vital metres as Balmamion, and the fabled pink jersey, disappeared up the road, floating away from *Parmigiano*. Adorni though, ever the warrior, gradually recovered his composure and, nothing more to lose, gave manful chase. Spotting a Carpano jersey in the middle distance he produced one more devastating, colossal effort and caught... Italo Zilioli.

In catching Zilioli Franco Balmamion had instructed his team-mate not to attempt to pace him (the Champion's form was so good that Zilioli couldn't have lived with him anyway) but to wait for Adorni, to act as quarry for the desperate pink jersey. When Adorni realized that the Carpano he was bearing down on was the wrong one, his morale, and his strength, deserted him completely.

Balmamion ultimately put the thick end of three minutes into the floundering, over-geared Adorni, reduced Taccone's winning margin to four minutes, and comfortably won a second consecutive Giro, once more without claiming a single stage-win. Working smarter, not harder.

La Gazzetta dello Sport recorded that, 'In truth Balmamion looked so fresh that he could in all probability begin the Giro again tomorrow and still win, so economically did he ride this one. His performance was absolutely masterful.'

Did he enjoy the second Giro more than the first?

'I enjoyed the *feeling* of it more. After the first Giro many people in the media said I was lucky, so I was determined to prove them wrong. It was a hard, pressurised Giro but I felt good throughout, always confident that if I could survive the time trial I would win. There is no doubt that Adorni made a big mistake in attacking me whilst wearing the maglia rosa, and some said he threw the race away. But for all his class I know that I won that Giro because I was the strongest, regardless of his errors that day. Of course there was a big debate in the press about it and some said that I wasn't a great winner because again I hadn't won a stage, but in truth I didn't care. Taccone and Adorni may have won the popularity contest, but my job was to win the Giro, and the reality is that I was the first since Coppi in 1953 to successfully defend it.'

`Returning in triumph to Nole Canavese after the 1963 Giro

SAINTS AND SINNERS, MONEY SPINNERS

'I'll be honest. Balmamion was a good rider. He won the Giro twice, but I think his time has passed. Thanks to his opportunism he can still be well placed in stage-races, but there are many better riders in Italy now.'

Vittorio Adorni, interview with *Miroir du Cyclisme*, May 1966

Balmamion and Giacotto disagreed strongly when the extravagantly talented Italo Zilioli, 'the new Coppi', disobeyed team orders at the Tre Valli Varesine single-day classic in August 1963. Though Zilioli ultimately won the race, he was thought by his team-mates to have ridden not for Carpano but for himself, not that Giacotto, infatuated by Zilioli's audacity and verve, could have cared less. Angered by Giacotto's intransigence, Balmamion signed an enormously lucrative one-year contract with the Swiss team CYNAR, another aperitif manufacturer keen to cash in on the thriving Italian market. There followed an injury-plagued, crash-ridden and ultimately miserable 1964 season, in which he finished a depressing eighth at the Giro and failed narrowly to win the Tour of Switzerland. For the 1965 season he was re-united with Giacotto, signing a two-year contract with Teofilo Sanson, a wealthy, cycling daft ice cream maker, originally from Verona but resident in Turin. Balmamion and Zilioli would spearhead Sanson's assault on cycling's great races, adhering to the principles of the now defunct Carpano.

Balmamion came agonizingly close to winning the 1965 Milan–San Remo. In a virtual carbon copy of the 1962 Milan–Torino he escaped with Vittorio Adorni, the two establishing a seemingly impregnable lead over the penultimate climb, the Capo Berta. Only this time Adorni, desperate to finally land a really big win following four pro seasons in which, despite several Giro stage-wins, he'd earned a reputation as a 'nearly man', opened negotiations to buy the win. Balmamion, though, had no particular need of the money. As a two-time winner of the Giro he was already wealthy beyond his wildest imaginings, and he, too, wanted to claim Italy's most prestigious single-day prize. As the horse-trading continued on and on the two began to dither, enabling the powerful Dutchman, Arie Den Hartog, to solo across the gap and make contact on the final climb, the Poggio. Adorni opened the sprint 300 metres from the line but it was no contest; Arie Den Hartog of Holland won the 56th Milan–San Remo. A cocked-up Franco Balmamion languished in third.

Thereafter Balmamion toiled for two fractured, disjointed seasons, during which he failed either to win a significant race or to secure a podium finish at his national tour, finishing fifth in 1965 and sixth the following year. Zilioli, already a runner-up behind Anquetil at the 1964 Giro, finished second twice more, as Franco, still in his mid-20s, settled prematurely into the role of *gregario di lusso* for the brilliant, fragile and ultimately unfulfilled Torinese.

Now Franco Balmamion, his best days seemingly already behind him at the age of only 27, signed a contract to ride in support of defending *maglia rosa,* Gianni Motta, at Molteni. It was the winter of 1966. Ostensibly a high class 'second wheel' for the prestigious 50th anniversary Giro, Balmamion, though evidently no longer thought capable of challenging for victory, offered Molteni the publicity value and prestige of being an ex-winner, the best mountain *gregario* in the race, and a cast iron top-ten finisher in the event that Motta, irascible and somewhat immature, might falter.

Come May, the silent former champion suffered his customary hunger-flat on the second stage, shipping four minutes to the favourites Gimondi, Adorni, Anquetil, Motta and the young Belgian sensation Eddy Merckx. He rallied well before losing a further two minutes on stage ten when obliged to give his bike to Motta, as the underperforming champion punctured towards the conclusion of the race. Motta, his training and diet controlled by a shady personal 'guru' figure, looked undernourished and exhausted throughout. He performed disastrously as Anquetil claimed the pink jersey on stage sixteen, a 45-kilometre time trial to Verona. The following day team-manager Albani finally gave Balmamion licence to attack and he promptly joined a group which put four minutes into the Frenchman. In his keenness finally to secure a first Giro stage-win, Balmamion contributed little to the break, eschewing an even greater time gain in saving himself for a sprint – which he predictably failed to win.

With Motta a spent force, the Molteni management now turned to Balmamion to salvage their Giro and, following a snow interrupted stage in the Dolomites, the Canavese increased the pressure by clawing back still more time with third place in the biggest mountain stage of the race. By the penultimate day Anquetil, by virtue of his customary supremacy against the watch, retained a 34-second lead over Gimondi, riding for the super wealthy Salvarani team. The resurgent Balmamion, the strongest climber in the race, stood third, a further 13 seconds adrift.

On a flat, innocuous section following the ascent of the Passo Tonale, Gimondi launched the attack that was to reward him with the *maglia rosa*, as the other GC contenders first eyed one another then watched as he disappeared. Gimondi thus time trialed his way to the first of his three Giro wins, taking over four minutes from a moribund peloton. Film of the stage shows a lead group, containing Balmamion, Motta, Adorni, Anquetil, his Tour de France winning *domestique* Lucien Aimar and the Spaniard Pérez-Francés, staring sheepishly at the asphalt, seemingly stuck to the road as Gimondi simply takes off, unhindered and unchallenged. It's all very odd to say the least.

As race leader, Anquetil would in normal circumstances be expected either to lead the chase or, in the event that he was suffering badly, to have his team-mate do so. Though Anquetil was undoubtedly a declining force by 1967, that neither he, the ultra strong Aimar, nor for that matter anybody else went after Gimondi, seems so utterly derelict that it's almost impossible not to suspect a cabal. Accounts of the day refer to a mysterious, ill defined 'holy alliance' between Italian teams, determined to ensure that one of their own – Gimondi – would prevail over the anti-hero, and twice previous winner, Anquetil. All of which suggests that Anquetil was the unwitting victim of an Italian coup, except that he didn't chase (and, by his own admission, loved money much more than winning bike races – unless, of course, Raymond Poulidor was present).

Vin Denson, a Giro regular, confirmed that for Anquetil and his Bic team there were rich pickings to be had at the race, which they naturally regarded as less relevant on a sporting level than their own tour. They could earn well if they won at the Giro, could earn fantastically well if they didn't. Vin tells stories of bungled wheel changes, incorrect gear ratios, a plethora of mechanical and logistical cockups, all of which seemed to be left behind by the time the team arrived at the business end of the season, the Tour de France. Anquetil and his team of quite superb *domestiques* raced to win in France, but rode principally for money elsewhere, and the cycling-daft Salvarani brothers, rich, publicity hungry kitchen manufacturers, had *very* deep pockets.

The final day of the Giro saw a split stage, first climbing to the tiny hillside chapel of the Madonna dell Ghisallo, the patron saint of cyclists, before the 68-kilometre procession into Milan. The morning section saw Balmamion overhaul Anquetil in finishing second behind the Spanish King of the Mountains, Aurelio Gonzalez. In so doing he reduced his deficit to Gimondi to 3'36", a good deal less than the time conceded apparently needlessly the day before. I asked Franco for his take on what had happened:

'It is what it is. I had to watch Anquetil, team orders. For some reason neither Aimar nor Anquetil went after Gimondi and my team-mate Motta chose not to help me. Nobody tried to follow, so Felice won the Giro. All I will say is that Anquetil earned a *lot* of money at that Giro. Draw your own conclusions.'

Here I detected, for the first time during the many hours we spent together, signs of irritation at the line of questioning. How best to rephrase it? In his opinion had the strongest man won the Giro?

'No, but as I say, it is what it is.'

Balmamion is a modest, phlegmatic man, not predisposed to recrimination or regret. He enjoyed his career, won some and lost a great many more. And yet the memory of the legendary, golden anniversary Giro clearly seems still to trouble him. Balmamion's answer hints at something deeper and more profound than the usual good luck/bad luck peaks and troughs which make up the professional roadman's career.

Prior to the 1967 season Balmamion had effectively been written off as a potential Giro winner, a fact implicit in his signing to ride with Motta at Molteni. Molteni paid very well, but in choosing them in preference to a smaller team offering less money, but outright leadership status, Balmamion appeared tacitly to accept that his winning days were behind him. Only if Motta was absent or misfiring would he be granted a free hand, and only then if the course profile was hilly, better suited to his characteristics than those of the strapping German, Rudi Altig, the expensively recruited reigning World Champion. What's more, a new generation of fabulously talented Italian riders had emerged in his wake.

Vittorio Adorni's imperious performance in winning the 1965 Giro had been a towering achievement, with three stage-wins and a huge overall margin of victory, over eleven minutes. As a contest it may have been boring, but it confirmed Adorni's status as a genuinely world-class racer, the most comprehensive and accomplished Giro winner since Coppi. Later that summer young Gimondi had amazed the cycling world by defeating the short priced favourite, Poulidor, to win the Tour de France at his first attempt. Motta, arguably the most naturally talented of all of the new brooms, and third behind Gimondi in the '65 Tour, had been similarly excellent in capturing the tough Giro of 1966, seven minutes ahead of sixth placed Balmamion. Elsewhere the perennial Giro bridesmaid, Zilioli, and the climber, Bitossi, each threatened a breakthrough victory. Now 1963, the year in which Balmamion not only won his second Giro, but began the Tour de France with genuine podium aspirations (he thought he had a good shot at second overall behind the 'unbeatable' Anquetil, but on stage three crashed on the cobbles of the north, badly smashing his head and legs) suddenly seemed an awfully long time ago.

The notion began to take hold, and in truth still holds today, that the early 60s had indeed seen a crisis in Italian cycling, notwithstanding the fact that Balmamion's 1963 Giro and the great 1964 struggle between Anquetil and Zilioli had been exhilarating races, eminently more interesting than those dominated by the two 'greats' Adorni and Motta. The feeling grew that with Nencini and Baldini in decline and with their immediate successors generally limited, Balmamion, workmanlike and astute, forgoing spectacular stage-wins in favour of the hardheaded, utilitarian imperative of winning the Giro, had been the best of a mediocre lot. This I suspect slightly needles Franco. It needles him not because he has any particular interest in the subjective, illusory business of comparison, less still because he envies Gimondi and Adorni the affluence and celebrity that cycling has afforded them. My guess is that ultimately Balmamion feels slightly cheated of respect. Though he would never be so immodest as to say so directly, he knows full well that he was the strongest rider at the 1967 Giro, and that politics and commercial interests, not another rider's superior sporting ability, cost him the race. He knows that, had he won the 1967 Giro d'Italia in front of Anquetil, Gimondi, Adorni and Motta, the cycling world would find it difficult to forget so easily the hard fought victories of '62 and '63. It would be very difficult to deny the excellence of a rider good enough to have won the Giro three times.

Six weeks on from the Giro, riding with virtually no meaningful support, he finished third in an unusually hard Tour de France, won by the talented but fragile Frenchman Roger Pingeon, but overshadowed completely by the death of Tom Simpson in the kiln that was Mont Ventoux.

With the re-introduction of national teams the Tour organizers sought to energise the race as a spectacle and to level the playing field – extending invitations to cycling underdogs like Great Britain and Germany. Three French teams took the start, along with two each from the stronger cycling nations of Italy, Belgium and Spain. Holland and a Swiss/Luxemburg combine completed the 130-strong peloton. The 'official' Italian selection led by Gimondi comprised seven of his expensively assembled Salvarani trade-team *gregari* and two talented riders from the excellent Filotex team. Balmamion, leader of the second Italian team – the so-called 'Primavera' – found himself saddled with a disparate, incoherent bunch drawn from no fewer than four trade teams, most of whom were, for a variety of reasons, all but useless as *gregari*. Cycling contracts back then were traditionally awarded after the Tour de France and a sizeable minority of the Primavera crew were in France attention seeking for new contracts or publicity seeking for existing employers, whose brands they were at liberty to emblazon on their 'national' jerseys. As everybody knows, publicity seeking team-mates are about as useful to a grand tour specialist as a wooden compass. Equally useless, though infinitely more forgivable, are team-mates without the requisite talent to stay close enough to the leader to be of any material help. Throw in a couple of half-arsed, demob happy types determined to abandon at the first available opportunity before picnicking their way across France with their sweethearts, and you have a pretty reasonable approximation of Franco Balmamion's team for the 1967 Tour.

Pingeon effectively secured his victory with a great ride over the cobbled roads of Northern France into Belgium on stage five. Ably assisted by two of Balmamion's Primavera colleagues, he slipped the peloton's malfunctioning net and escaped to a six and a half minute advantage on the other favourites, a racing disaster which Balmamion still laments to this day:

'My team was a shambles, while Gimondi's wouldn't co-operate with us. We should have been working together, but instead they chose not to. We never collaborated at all and both Felice and I suffered as a result. Ridiculous.'

Though he graciously acknowledges Pingeon's audacity and subsequent strength and fortitude in winning the race, Balmamion recognises fully that he had the form of his life and that he could, probably should, have won a Tour well suited to his consistency and to his prodigious climbing ability. Gimondi, leader of the powerful Italian A team and pre-race favourite following his success at the Giro, won one stage before succumbing to gastroentiritis. Although he recovered to win a second stage, he finished a disappointing seventh overall.

I asked Balmamion whether the sadness he felt following Simpson's death had overshadowed the satisfaction of having finally ridden a good Tour de France:

'At the time everybody was destroyed. Personally I felt totally crushed by it because I'd liked and admired him greatly. Simpson had been ill for quite a few days. I could see that when he was dropped on the Ballon d'Alsace on stage eight, he already looked pretty terrible, like a ghost. But he was an unbelievable fighter and some said he needed a good tour to earn a good contract, though I'd heard he might be going to Salvarani with Gimondi. But it's cycling, the show must go on. So yes, it was shocking for us all, and I suppose it should have changed things, though ultimately we knew it wouldn't and couldn't. The reality is that Simpson's death changed absolutely nothing.'

Lucien Aimar leads Jan Janssen, Tom Simpson and Balmamion on the Ballon d'Alsace, Tour de France, 1967

Guido Neri said that if the Italian team had been united Franco could have won the 1967 Tour. True?

'It's like it is. Pingeon won the Tour in one stage and that's fair enough. The French team was very strong to support him, and we were very disorganised, very weak.'

The following week, at the single-day Tour of Tuscany, Franco Balmamion, briefly once more Italy's best cyclist, became National Champion, riding away from a group of 12 containing, amongst others, Adorni, Gimondi and Motta, the cream of Italy's second golden generation. No obvious politics, little by way of team strategy, 94 athletes on a relentlessly hard, hilly 256-kilometre course, under the baking Tuscan sun. Balmamion attacked 40 kilometres from the finish to win comfortably and well, by the best part of four minutes – a dividend for the best season of his career. Only rather perplexingly, when I enquire about his capture of the fabled *maglia tricolore*, Franco Balmamion becomes a little vague, simultaneously avoiding the question and telling me the answer, 'I was in great form that summer. I probably wouldn't have won Tuscany if I'd won the Giro.' All of which leads me to speculate, not for the first time, that in the murky, secretive world of professional cycling two and two can, and quite often do, add up to five. A *maglia rosa* for a *maglia tricolore*?

Balmamion would continue to ride professionally for a further five years. He did a decent enough Giro in finishing seventh as Merckx annihilated the peloton in 1968, then spent two injury-affected, winless and largely unhappy years working for Gimondi at Salvarani, before joining their great kitchen making rival SCIC. He retired from the sport in 1972. Thereafter, he set up in business selling and maintaining bar games and concentrated his efforts on being a good husband to Rosanna, an attentive father to Mauro and Silvia.

'I'd had enough. I could have done another couple of years, but professional cycling is no career for a father of two. I became concerned about the consequences should I crash, and nervous when riding on wet roads. I decided I wanted to be with my family.'

Approaching his 70th year he continues to work part-time ('as a social exercise') and still lives unpretentiously, though very well, in

Cirie, just a few kilometres along the way from Nole Canavese. For his charity, modesty and humility he was recently voted 'National Grandfather of the Year' by the Lions Club of Italy.

National Road-race Champion 1967

Grandfather of the Year, 2007

WOULD HAVE, COULD HAVE, SHOULD HAVE

Vito Taccone's devastating climbing performance at the 1963 Giro proved to be the apogee of a career which promised much, but which, despite a catalogue of misadventures and near misses, never really delivered. He won the Tour of Tuscany later that summer, before hilariously claiming his fifteen minutes of fame at the 1964 Tour de France. Accused by several riders of causing crashes in the peloton as he sprinted erratically towards stage finishes, little Taccone clouted the gangly Spaniard Fernando Manzaneque, and was ejected from the race, securing his place at the top table of climbing fruitcakes. He then proceeded to boycott the Tour for the rest of his career, a shame for his legion of supporters. The more so because the French, once they'd recovered from the collective laughing fit induced by the sight of little Taccone being swatted by the giant Manzaneque, couldn't have cared less. God love 'em.

Though he would win mountain stages in subsequent Giri, Taccone never truly animated the race, failing to reach the podium in seven further attempts. Towards the end of his career, painfully aware now of his shortcomings as a grand tour rider, the Abruzzese focussed his attention on single-day races, in particular the Italian National Championship. Here too he was to be frustrated. Beaten into third by Italo Zilioli and the prolific sprinter, Michele Dancelli, in the 1966 event held in hilly Lazio, Taccone then finished a distant second to the all-powerful Gimondi in the 1968 edition. Still more misery the following year in the mountains of Calabria, the toe-end of Italy's boot, as Taccone agonizingly lost a two-man sprint to Vittorio Adorni, by then an outstanding World Champion. Following the race Adorni, outraged by Taccone's gamesmanship, clouted him around the head with his bike pump. By the time the Chamois of Abruzzo, the most rancorous and by some distance the least popular of the class of '62, called time on his career in 1970, he had few friends in the peloton.

Upon retirement Taccone set up a business making spirits before moving into the manufacture of sportswear, specialising in cycling clothing. In 1973 he was amongst a gang of 11 caught brawling in Avezzano's city centre and found guilty of affray. Thereafter, trouble seemed to follow him doggedly around, much as it had during his cycling career. In 1982 he was sentenced to three years imprisonment for GBH, serving twenty-one months before receiving parole. Three years later Taccone was arrested again, this time following a police raid on an illegal gambling den in Avezzano. Later, he survived cancer, then dabbled in local politics as a councillor for the nefarious right wing PRI party, retiring from the sportswear business in 2006. In June 2007 he found himself once more in handcuffs, arrested this time on suspicion of manufacturing and distributing counterfeit and/or stolen designer clothing. He remained a contentious figure in his home town, still polarising opinion as he neared his 70th year. Some amongst the *Avezzanesi* believed him to be a loveable rogue, stupid and misguided, but ultimately harmless. Sadly, a great many more saw in him a vicious, greedy little criminal, a national embarrassment for a beautiful region fighting hard to rid itself of a centuries old reputation for ignorance and tribalism.

Not one of the riders I interviewed for this book had a kind word for him. When I asked Antonio Bailetti for his thoughts on Taccone, Bailetti, a gentle man not at all predisposed to animosity, simply answered 'Zero'. For his part, Balmamion politely stated that he 'always tried not to speak badly of anybody and is not about to start now'.

Despite several assurances from his beleaguered wife, I was unable ultimately to pin Taccone down to arrange a meeting, a pity since Imerio Massignan had asked me to call in a 40-year-old debt. Vito Taccone died in October 2007.

Taccone's rival and fellow Avezzano, **Vincenzo Meco**, considered the revelation of the '62 Giro, would fall spectacularly from grace. Tipped for stardom following his audacious performances here, he endured a fruitless, injury plagued 1963. Appointed team-leader at the Vuelta, Meco failed to finish as Anquetil became the first rider in history to claim all three Grand Tours. The Abruzzese rode an undistinguished first week of the Giro, before climbing off as his form, and with it his season, disintegrated. He began the following year with a promising third place at the Trofeo Laiguellia, won by Guido Neri, but it proved to be a false dawn. Meco abandoned the Giro, and would abandon again the following year, too. For a further three seasons he found team managers willing to gamble that he might rediscover his 1962 form, but it was a hopeless, futile endeavour as Meco's downward spiral continued. He never again won a professional race, failed even to earn selection for the Giro, before professional cycling finally ran out of faith in him in 1967. The following year a disillusioned Meco emigrated to Canada, joining the huge Abruzzese community in Quebec. Here he rediscovered himself as an amateur cyclist and enjoyed an outstanding career in winning, amongst others, successive editions of the prestigious Montreal–Quebec classic. In 2000 he was inducted into the Quebecois Cycling hall of fame. At 67, Meco still loves his bike and rides over 10,000 kilometres a year.

Imerio Massignan finally parted company with Legnano at the conclusion of the 1963 season – destination Carpano. With Balmamion departed, Giacotto looked to Massignan and the precociously talented Italo Zilioli to contest the Giro. Sadly it wasn't to be. A kidney infection in February put paid to his first season and Giacotto, true to form, didn't renew his contract at the season's end. Thereafter, Imerio never truly rediscovered the snap and sparkle which saw him briefly eclipse Charly Gaul as the best climber in the world. Like many of his generation Massignan was a spent force well before his 30th birthday. He moved to Liguria and opened a tobacconist close to the coast, before settling in Piedmont where he set up a business installing industrial flooring. Now retired and well into his 70s, Imerio Massignan still rides today. With Francesco Moser he recently went back to, and rode over the terrible, mythical Gavia for charity. To a generation of Italian cycling fans he remains an iconic, unforgettable figure, the Spider of the Dolomites.

Like his close friend Massignan, **Graziano Battistini** never again found the endurance required to threaten the Giro. Though he persisted until 1968, ultimately Battistini was unable to recover well enough to mount further challenges, as a new generation headed by Vittorio Adorni, Gianni Motta and Felice Gimondi came to the fore. Like Massignan he regretted his misplaced loyalty to Pavesi and Legnano, with whom he stayed, despite a lucrative offer from Rik Van Looy's wealthy Faema team. Following his collapse in the closing stages of the 1962 Giro, he would win only one more race of any real note, a Dolomite stage contested in a horrendous blizzard at the 1965 edition of the race. Following retirement, Battistini opened a small chain of clothing stores on the Ligurian coast and helped to nurture gifted local riders, one of whom, Massimo Podenzana, would twice become national champion in the mid-1990s. A shy, unpretentious man who loved nothing more than the company of his family and to spend time on his smallholding, Graziano Battistini was diagnosed with stomach cancer in October 1993 and died three short months later, aged only 57.

The Flemish hard man, **Armand Desmet,** followed his outstanding performance at the Giro with an impressive fifth overall in the 1963 Tour de France before his powers began to decline the following season, a veteran aged just 32. He carried on riding for a further four seasons and still won the occasional race, but they were mainly low-key criteriums in Flanders, nothing remotely as significant as his exemplary, ultimately heartbreaking ride in the Giro of 1962. Speeding home late one night in the winter of 1967, Desmet was stopped and searched by an over zealous traffic cop. The search revealed several 'illicit drugs'. With the introduction of new, draconian laws in Belgium in the wake of the Simpson disaster, Armand Desmet found himself criminalised simply for, as he saw it, carrying the tools of the professional cyclist's trade, for doing his job. He received a two-year ban from competing in Belgium, an inglorious end to a distinguished career largely spent serving Van Looy, the most ruthless, least grateful of all of cycling's autocrats. The two would not speak for 20 years.

In 1969 Desmet opened the bike shop he would run for many years, before his health, in common with many riders from his generation, began to deteriorate prematurely. Recently the town of Waregem honoured his sporting excellence with a gala weekend, and organised a reunion of his old team-mates. Aged 76, Desmet's health has stabilised somewhat, though he remains a fragile figure, scarcely recognisable as the warrior who illuminated the first fortnight of the Giro. He is cared for by, amongst others, his son Tom, formerly a moderately successful professional bike rider.

Nino Defilippis departed Carpano in acrimonious circumstances at the conclusion of an unremarkable 1963 season, which saw him claim only one win, the aforementioned Giro stage. Unable to reconcile his differences with the team, he received a terse, in his own words 'glacial', letter from Attilio Turati stating simply that Carpano would not be renewing his contract. Nino signed a one-year deal with the newly formed I.B.A.C. team, managed by fellow Torinese Pino Favero, sharing leadership duties with Graziano Battistini. Nino again secured a stage at the Giro, but with his powers fading chose retirement over mediocrity, aged 32.

Appointed manager of the Italian national team for the 1973 World Championship Road-race at Barcelona, Defilippis faced ridicule in the press over his controversial decision to omit the gifted but controversial Milanese champion, Gianni Motta, from his team. Nino gambled his reputation in placing the entire team at the disposal of Gimondi, reasoning that only in uniting a powerful team behind a single leader could he hope to upset the great Merckx. The ploy paid handsome dividends, as the Belgians self-destructed amidst a venomous row between Merckx and the brilliant, cocky Flemish sprinter, Freddy Maertens, in the closing stages. Regardless of the Merckx/Maertens polemic Nino's decision to discard Motta is now recognised as one of the tactical masterstrokes of the era. The following year Nino's team, featuring amongst others Gimondi, the 1972 Champion, Marino Basso, and the great Franco Bitossi appeared, on paper at least, the strongest ever assembled by the Azzuri. This time, however, Merckx took matters into his own hands, demolishing the field in becoming the first to complete the 'impossible' Giro/Tour/Worlds treble.

In 1995 Defilippis, as successful in business as he'd been in cycling, had an idea. He would take it upon himself to raise £250,000, his intention being to erect a monument in honour of Piedmont's greatest ever sportsman, Fausto Coppi. Nino, in tandem with his great friend Angelo Marello, not only lobbied tirelessly for the project, but contributed a significant sum of his own money. The ten-metre bronze sculpture by Giuseppe Tarantino, in the gardens overlooking Walter Martin's Velodrome, evokes the golden era of cycling, with references to Coppi's proudest achievements and to the great climbs of the Dolomites and Alps, the cornerstones of the Giro d'Italia. The work is intended to serve as a reminder, not only of Coppi's career, but of the fraternity and camaraderie that sport, even top level sport, can engender. Amongst a select band of honoured guests at the unveiling in June 2002 were five outstanding former cyclists in Gimondi, Merckx, Fiorenzo Magni, Raphael Geminiani and a beaming Franco Balmamion – proof, if proof were needed, of the restorative, redemptive powers of riding a bicycle. Powers that today's Grand Tour fraudsters, adrift in a sea of greed and avarice with their re-formed blood and synthetic hormones, would do well to remember if cycling is to survive. As professional cycling staggers punch-drunk towards an abyss entirely of its own making, it shames the memory of the golden age, shames the memory of Tom Simpson, shames the memory of Fausto Coppi.

Nino and Franco remain great friends.

THE SILENT CHAMPION

Those charged with chronicling the history of cycling's great races necessarily characterise the passing eras by the great winners and losers who defined them. The unforgettable postwar saga of Coppi against Bartali, Bobet's consummate domination of the Tour de France in the early 50s, followed by the two brilliant climbers Gaul and Bahamontes, hammer and tongs in the Pyrenees. The early-60s brought Anquetil's caustic, one-sided rivalry with Raymond Poulidor at the Tour, before the extraordinary, insatiable Merckx sucked the life from the race, and from the Giro, during the late-60s and early-70s. In recent years the great Spaniard, Miguel Induraín and an American, Lance Armstrong, phenomenal athletes backed by powerful teams, have bestrode the Tour de France, shackling an impotent peloton, killing the race as a contest and rendering the world's greatest sporting event for the most part colourless and drab. Cycling's harsh but irrefutable truth is that, all too often, her greatest Grand Tour riders have been responsible for some of the most anodyne, featureless stage-racing in history.

The Italian cycling community, parochial and romantic (the country in microcosm, in fact) fondly recalls not only the Coppi/Magni/Bartali Giri but Gaul's two wonderful triumphs of 1956 and 1959, sandwiched as they were by those of the irrepressible Gastone Nencini and the dazzling, fluent Ercole Baldini. Vito Taccone's astonishing feat in capturing five mountain stages at the 1963 Giro is, with good reason, the stuff of legend, whilst Anquetil, a two time *maglia rosa*, is revered for his supremacy against the watch. The mid-60s are synonymous with the emergence of an outstanding generation of riders led by Zilioli, Motta and Adorni, succeeded by the Tuscan Bitossi, Michele Dancelli and Felice Gimondi, later Italy's 'Anti–Merckx'. Following Merckx's strangulation of both the Giro and Milan–San Remo (which he won a staggering seven times) the introvert Piedmontese Giuseppe Saronni and his elegant, handsome nemesis Francesco Moser recalled the golden age with a wonderfully splenetic head-to-head, tit-for-tat rivalry which. between 1975 and 1984, saw each claim their nation's great triptych – Milan–San Remo, the Giro and the Tour of Lombardia

– as well as the World Championship. During the eighties the fearsome Breton Bernard Hinault, and his countryman and fellow Tour de France winner, Laurent Fignon, each crossed the Alps to ridicule Italy's finest before Induraín's matter of fact, shelling peas double of the early nineties. In recent times, with the Giro traipsing grudgingly towards globalization, winners have emerged from all corners: Irish, American, even a pair of extravagantly talented Russians have emerged triumphant from the great race. Unloved – and in Hinault's case despised – they may have been, but all have their place in Giro folklore, all are admired for their brilliance and strength of character, prerequisites both for a grand tour winner.

Lost somewhere amidst all the revelry and myth-making is the story of a rider not possessed of Gaul's virtuosity, Taccone's gambling instinct, Nencini's never-say-die belligerence. He never annihilated the peloton as Adorni did in 1965, never time trialed with Baldini's immense grace and power, nor beguiled the Italian sporting public as the swashbuckling Marco Pantani would in the late-90s. Where Nino Defilippis helped himself to nine Giro stages, Franco Balmamion won successive *maglie rose* without once crossing the line first, not that winning stages ultimately has anything to do with winning stage-races. While Gimondi, Moser and Defilippis quite properly found fortune basking in the afterglow of their exemplary careers, Balmamion slipped quietly away from cycling, into the company of his own and into the world of family and hard work. This cyclist, whose Giro record surpassed all but the very best, whose extraordinary mental and physical *courage* in winning the 1962 edition was at least the equal of anything achieved by any of the above, remains an obscure, forgotten figure. How, then, has cycling contrived to disregard the achievements of a rider who, with a fair wind and a fraction of the support offered to Gimondi, might well have won, not only a third Giro, but also the Tour de France? How?

Italy, it goes without saying, is a beautiful, diverse, eclectic country. Though railing endlessly against the state is evidently a national obsession, the Italians, unlike say the English, in general retain a profound attachment to and pride in their *Bel Paese*, their 'beautiful land'. In Italy, style – or at least the appearance of style – invariably trumps crude, prosaic substance. This overly developed sense of the aesthetic is made manifest, not only in the ways Italians dress, present and behave themselves, but in the food they eat, in the products they design and manufacture, in the municipal buildings and cities they inhabit. Conversely, it's one of the reasons why the Banks and public offices are so hopelessly unwieldy, the politics so impenetrable and compromised, why the myriad police forces (Carabinieri, Penitentiary, Finance, State Police, even amongst the plethora of uniformed jobsworths, the 'Forestry Police') are so immaculately turned out, so utterly officious and incompetent. The Italians, for whom the collective is everything, even have a collective verb for the creation of all things bright and beautiful. To create the correct impression is *fare bella figura*, literally 'to make a beautiful figure'. Though subjective, the *bella figura* is applicable, not only to the design and outward appearance of a person or object, but to a behavioural code that is, broadly speaking, mannered, politic and conformist. Most of the Italians I know, in particular those of the Centre and North, for all their complaining and gesticulating and in spite of their gift for polemic and plain old fashioned *loudness*, are essentially conformist by nature.

Herein, or rather hereout, I believe lies the reason for Balmamion's continued anonymity. Unusually for a high profile professional athlete – and to his eternal credit, – Franco Balmamion was unequivocally and unashamedly no *bella figura*, either on or off a bicycle. That he made no *bella figura* on the bike should come as no great surprise. Balmamion's inability to make the *bella figura*, to the best of my knowledge and his, never hindered him unduly in his quest to ride his bicycle over big mountains more quickly, more often than the next man. That Balmamion was amongst the best bike handlers, climbers and descenders of his generation was not due in any way to his ability or otherwise to look sophisticated in a sharp suit, or to dazzle journalists with his loquacious insights into the minutiae of stage-racing tactics. He saved his formidable cycling intellect for cycling, specifically for winning bike races. The *bella figura*, in common with extravagant displays of those other Italian male staples, posturing and self-aggrandisement, never counted for a great deal in the Lanzo Valley. You couldn't bank it, and it certainly never helped anyone win the Giro d'Italia. Cycling's beauty lies not in the fluidity and colour of a fast moving peloton, nor in the mesmeric fluency of elegant pedal strokes. The true beauty of the sport, the real *bella figura*, is to be found elsewhere, in the ugly, human brutality of sufferance.

Though he clearly enjoys reminiscing about the period in which he was a cyclist, Balmamion conscientiously avoids referring to his own achievements, so much so that when pressed he relates them purely as matters of fact. This is no false modesty on his part, for Franco knows he was an exceptional racer, particularly in confounding the cycling *cognoscenti* when returning to the top of the sport in 1967. I think he simply finds the idea that his career might bestow upon him some degree of celebrity embarrassing, unfathomable, distasteful even.

For eleven years between 1961 and 1972 Franco Balmamion, the silent champion of Nole Canavese, was simply a racing cyclist, intermittently brilliant, for the most part very good, sometimes by his own admission mediocre. For three weeks in the early summer of 1962, despite overwhelming odds to the contrary, he was the best, the hardest, the bravest cyclist in Italy. But still just a cyclist, no more and no less.

Franco Balmamion's Professional Palmarès

1961 (Bianchi)

3rd Tour of d'Emilie
3rd GP d'Orte
4th GP Chignolo Po
7th Tour of Veneto
20th Tour of Italy
    2nd Stage 1
    4th Stage 19

1962 (Carpano)

1st Giro d'Italia
    2nd Stage 16
    3rd Stage 4
    4th Stage 20
    8th Stage 10
    8th Stage 14
1st Milan–Turin
1st Tour of the Appennines
1st GP Parisien (TTT)
2nd Circuit Maggiore
2nd Tour of Switzerland
    2nd Points Competition
    2nd Stage 3,
    3rd Stage 4,
    6th Stage 5
3rd Cicuit of the 3 Valleys
        Varesines
3rd Targa d'Oro
4th Tour of Veneto
8th Trophy Super Prestige Pernod
11th Tour of Emilie
12th Tour of Piedmont
16th Tour of Lombardy

1963 (Carpano)

1st Giro d'Italia
    3rd Stage 11
    3rd Stage 13
    3rd Stage 18
    3rd Stage 19
    5th Stage 12
    9th Stage 1 Stage,
    10th Stage 7
    1st Team Prize
1st Championship of Zurich
3rd Tour of Veneto
6th Tour of the Appenines
7th Milan–San Remo
9th Circuit of the 3 Valleys
        Varesines
10th GP Vignola
15th Coppa Bernocchi
Abandoned Tour de France
(Crashed)
Voted most unlucky rider of Tour.

1964 (Cynar)

2nd Tour of Switzerland
    2nd King of Mountains
    2nd Stage 3
    5th Stage 5
    10th Stage 6*
2nd GP Parisien
3rd Tour of the Appennines
6th Tour of Romagna
6th Coppa Sabatini
6th GP Lugano (TT)
7th Tour of Romandie
    3rd Stage 1*

8th Giro d'Italia
   5th Stage 21
   8th Stage 8
   9th Stages 12
   9th Stage 17
   10th Stage 10
10th Italian RR Championships
10th Coppa Agostoni

*NB. Franco rode for Swiss star
Rolf Maurer as his Swiss sponsors
wanted.

1965 (Sanson)

1st Caen (TTT with Zilioli)
2nd Cirie (Criterium)
3rd Milan–San Remo
3rd Tour of Latium
3rd Genoa–Nice
4th GP Moltini
5th Tour of Abruzzo
5th GP Robbiano
5th Giro d'Italia
   4th Stage 13 (TT)
   5th Stage 18
   7th Stage 20
   8th Stage 3
5th Trophy Mattoetti
6th Tour of Veneto
7th Varese
7th Circuit of the 3 Valleys
      Varesines
8th World Championships
9th GP Sormano
9th Tour of Romagne
11th Tour of the Apennines
13th Italian RR Championships

1966 (Sanson)

1st Circuit Maggiora
1st Cirie (Criterium France)
2nd La Cronostaffetta (3-Stage
Mountain race, results based on best
3 riders)
4th Tour of Switzerland
   2nd King of Mountains
   4th Stage 2
   5th Stage 3
   7th Stage 6
4th Tour of Tessin
4th GP Robbiano
6th Giro d'Italia
   7th Stage 17
   8th Stage 20
   9th Stage 13 (TT)
   9th Stage 19
   10th Stage 14
6th Tour of Campanie
8th Tour of Tuscany
8th Milan–San Remo
8th Torino–Adriatico
8th Tour of Veneto
15th Italian Championships

1967 (Molteni)

1st Italian RR Championship.
1st Circuit Maggiora
2nd Giro d'Italia
   2nd Stage 17
   2nd Stage 22a
   3rd Stage
   3rd Stage 20
   10th Stage 16 (TT)
3rd Tour de France
   2nd King of Mountains
   2nd Stage 8
   4th Stage 13
   5th Stage 16

6th Stage 10
7th Stage 20
8th Stage 1a (Prologue TT)
4th Coppa Bernocchi
8th Tour of Romandie
   2nd Stage 4
8th Tour of Latium
9th Circuit of the 3 Vallys
   Varesines
30th World Championships

1968 (Molteni)

1st Team La Cronostaffetta
   3rd Stage 1
5th Italian Championships
8th Giro d'Italia
   7th Stage 5
   10th Stage 9
   15th Stage 12
11th Milan–Turin
11th Tour of Tuscany
12th= Championship of Zurich
18th Circuit of the 3 Valleys
   Varesines

1969 (Salvarani)

1st .GP. Camors (Crit France)
1st Circuit Maggiora
1st Stage 5a (TTT) Paris–Nice
1st Team overall. Paris–Nice
6th GP Forli TT
13th Italian RR Championship
39th Tour de France
   3rd Stage 1b
   4th Stage 2

1970 (Salvarani)

1st Prologue TTT Tour of
   Romandie
3rd Tour of Piedmont
12th Tour de France
12th Giro d'Italia
13th Italian RR Championship.
28th GP Frankfurt.

1971 (Scic)

Abandoned Giro d'Italia
3rd Prologue (TTT)
9th Stage 1
Abandoned Tour de France
7th Capriata d'Orba
8th Belmonte Piceno
17th Flèche Wallonne

1972 (Scic)

2nd Prologue TTT Tour of
   Switzerland
8th Coppa Agostini
9th Trophy Matteotti
13th Italian RR Championship.
21st Tour of Switzerland
38th Giro d'Italia

Compiled by Richard Allchin and
Mick Clark

Other books published by
Mousehold Press and Sport and Publicity

Mr Tom: the true story of Tom Simpson
Chris Sidwells

Master Jacques: the enigma of Jacques Anquetil
Richard Yates

Golden Stages of the Tour de France
edited by Richard Allchin and Adrian Bell

A Peiper's Tale
Allan Peiper with Chris Sidwells

Viva la Vuelta!
Lucy Fallon & Adrian Ball

In Pursuit of Stardom
Tony Hewson

This Island Race: inside 135 years of British bike-racing
Les Woodland

From the Pen of J. B. Wadley
selected and edited by Adrian Bell

The Sweat of the Gods
Benjo Maso (translated by Michiel Horn)

Wheels along the Waveney; a history of the Godric Cycling Club
Tim Hilton

The Eagle of the Canavese: Franco Balmamion and the Giro d'Italia
Herbie Sykes

Tomorrow, we ride…
Jean Bobet (translated by Adam Berry)

A Racing Cyclist's Worst Nightmare
Tony Hewson

Lapize: now there was an ace
Jean Bobet (translated by Adam Berry)

Brian Robinson: Pioneer
Graeme Fife

Also available only from Sport and Publicity:

21 Years of Cycling Photography
Phil O'Connor

Ride and be Damned: the glory years of the British League of Racing Cyclists
Chas Messenger